THE
MAGICAL CHILD
WITHIN YOU

THE
MAGICAL CHILD
WITHIN YOU

Bruce Davis, Ph.D.
Illustrations by Genny Davis

CELESTIALARTS
Berkeley, California

Previously published by Inner Light Books & Tapes
                        21 Crest Road
                        Fairfax, CA 94930

                        ISBN 0-911717-00-5

Currently published by Celestial Arts
                       P.O. Box 7327
                       Berkeley, CA 94707

Cover Design by: Ken Scott
Typographer: HMS Typography, Inc.

Current Library of Congress Cataloging in Publication Data

Davis, Bruce, 1950–
    The magical child within you.
    82-084601

ISBN 0-89087-422-0

9 — 88

Contents

Introduction

There is a child within each of us crying out:

"Listen! I am sick and tired of being ignored day after day. You go to work, out with your friends, to sleep, to eat, live your life as if I do not exist. Every once in a while you notice me when you are depressed or home sick in bed. But do you really care about me? Do you really ask what I want?

Here I am sitting around waiting, forever waiting for you to recognize me. First your parents began ignoring parts of me and gradually you continued where your parents left off.

Remember me? I am your feelings, your dreams and fantasies. I am the one who used to enjoy going to the park. I am the one who likes pizza, candy, mountains, sunshine, and who wants to play. I am also the one who likes to be held and told he is loved. I am the child within you, *I am you.*

I don't care if you are an adult now. Why does that mean you have to forget about me? Why can't adults enjoy themselves as children do? Why must being an adult mean that the child in you must try not to exist?

Believe me, living in your adult world of constant struggle, is not easy. How do you think I feel when you stuff me with lots of food during dinner while you talk with your important friends, people you really don't like?

Where am I supposed to go when I am angry and you don't recognize me? Then you wonder why you have indigestion or weight problems.

Where do you think your problems come from?

I know you need your important friends. I know you

have to make a living. I know you have to take care of others. But have you ever thought if you really became *my* friend, you wouldn't need some things from others so much?

Have you ever thought that if you took care of your feelings and appreciated your little desires that you wouldn't need so much income to appease me? Have you ever thought that if you were nicer to *yourself*, taking care of others would not be so much of a burden?

I know you are trying to get a better position so you will have more time to be with me. I have felt the different therapies you have tried which reintroduce you to parts of me. But I want you to know *all* of me. I am tired of others pushing and shoving, fishing around for me. I want you to know *me*.

I don't expect you to change overnight. I have been waiting for you to recognize me long enough. To be honest, a part of me will never understand how you can treat me the way you do. Why is it so difficult for you to be as you want?

If I was literally your child, you would listen to me and care how I am. Well, I am literally *your child*, you have just learned not to see *me*."

This book is about the process of raising the child inside of me into the world. The following pages are for you and the child within you. This book shares my path, to be taken at a momentary glance, paragraph, or chapter. Like any path just take it and be with it as you wish. For some perhaps just the pictures are right. For everyone I encourage the most self-ish part of you to pick up the book, put it down, to smile at it, or fight it exactly as you want.

I have found hundreds of theories explaining nearly everything about being human. Similarly, I have seen and heard of dozens and dozens of techniques for raising children to become people and for changing people who are not happy after being raised. But I have always wanted something beyond merely learning to trust and to live someone else's theory and techniques. I have wanted to find my own way and relearn to trust it and to live it. If you share similar wishes, perhaps this book can be a guide and a friend.

The Garden's Path

I see myself walking down a path. Every few feet there are other roads with various promises if I would follow them. But I do not want to. I want to stay on this path. Everything is not perfect but at least this way I am choosing my own course.

There are many jobs, many relationships, many roads with lots of benefits. I could follow them, letting my feelings build and scream inside. I could try to pretend the pain is not there, keeping my sight on the benefits instead. But I seem to always lose. I lose a special part of myself. Even now a part of me is still screaming for all the feelings and desires I have had which were not experienced and appreciated in the past. I have found the best thing to do about the past and the present is to begin developing a path of my own will.

Everyday I am learning to plan my way from my own heart. This means looking for my heart instead of searching for the hearts of others. I don't care about other people any less. By listening to my own heart, I have simply found I have more to give when I want to give.

Following my own way I sometimes feel different, as if something is wrong with me. I can doubt myself and begin to struggle to make my path seem like others, or I can ask myself, "Is this path worthy of my life right now?" If it is, I want to do everything I can to take care of it.

Sometimes it seems my path
   is very different from everyone else's.
Now I can doubt myself and begin to struggle
   to make my path appear as theirs.
Or I can ask myself: "Is this path worthy
   of my life right now?"
And if it is, I want to do everything I can
   to take care of it.

It is not easy to live the path of my heart. But the child part of me has convinced me that it is even less easy to try to live the way of someone else's. I have been taught to conform to the ways of so many others that sometimes I don't even know what is mine, what I want. I have let others make decisions for me for so long, I cannot make choices myself. Parents, teachers and therapists have told me who I am until I am not certain what is me and what is not. I try to get back, making everyone responsible for how I am, instead of becoming responsible, beginning to respond to myself.

10

I am often looking for something to trust almost anywhere. I will let any path do my thinking for me as long as I can trust that it will make me feel better. At these times I am looking for my head, my heart, and my child, everywhere but where they are, within me.

Sometimes I feel the world has been telling me for so long what I feel and what I know that a path that is entirely my own seems impossible. On the other hand, once in a while, on a sudden hunch, I see something I want and I change my ways to reach for it. No matter how much my routines, my thoughts, and my feelings seem to belong to others, suddenly by noticing my desires, I begin living my life for *me*.

Something begins surging inside of me. I call it my child. I feel excited and safe. Something inside begins growing again. A spirit, an energy which is my own begins running through all of me. The more I make room and plan my life around this special part of myself, the more amazing this feeling becomes. My child feels unleashed into the world. I begin looking and living the way I am inside.

Before my head or my thoughts can be my own, I must know my child, my feelings. By developing the path of my heart, trusting my own will to unfold, my head, heart, and child become one, *me*. All the warmth and security, pleasure and happiness I have searched for out in the world are found inside. Everything seems to be waiting inside if I will only recognize it.

The garden I want to live in is no further than I am from myself. The whole thing is waiting for me to begin loving my heart and child, my will and feelings. Meanwhile I can continue allowing others to control me and control others in return. Or I can become my own controller, my own director. Instead of accepting or rejecting the ways of others, I begin accepting and rejecting my own ways until I find what I want. I begin raising the child within me, realizing myself in the world. The garden's path is found to be loving my child wherever I am. The seeds and the sunshine seem to be unlimited.

I know the only path in the world
That is for me is the one through my heart.
But sometimes I feel my heart is empty.
Now I can return to looking for someone else's path
And hope it will satisfy me or I can choose
A path in search of my heart.

Loving
My
Child

As with many people, instead of being raised to realize the love, success, and wealth I had inside, I was raised to believe love, success, and wealth were something out in the world I had to achieve. This course controlled and limited me in appreciating myself. My teachers, instead of trusting and supporting me to explore, play, and create the hundreds of ways for me to be five, nine, or nineteen, structured my days for me to learn and perform as they did and as they expected people my age to be. As an adult once again, there are many teachers who are ready to structure or define my days whether it is in business, therapy, school, or church. The opportunity for me to appreciate the hundreds of ways for me to be me is more rare. The chance for me to find my own way, my own edges and boundaries is not as easy to find.

When I look around me I see that most people have never had their own will or truly created their own way. To take away their structured lives and ask them to be who they want to be is unimaginable. Most everyone is either working or learning, married or single, and their life's experience somehow is fitted into a set of normally accepted categories. People having difficulty adjusting to the paved roads their lives are to take, seem either to live continually adjusting and changing roads or they are seeking another way, this one perhaps more of their own.

No matter how many or which path I chose to try, something was missing. The love and success I was searching for, seemed always just beyond my reach. At this point I decided to stop my world and look at it again. In the past when I had this feeling I would either try to ignore it or begin looking for a new relationship. Perhaps I would start a new project. I would begin reading and practicing some new techniques which were supposed to bring me closer to myself. When I looked around me I saw everyone doing the same or settling down, raising children, trying to give them what they always wanted for themselves.

Upon seeing my alternatives, I thought, why not begin giving to myself? Instead of raising a new child in the world, why not begin looking at the forgotten child in me and give him what he needs? Instead of starting a new project or new relationship, why not start a new relationship with myself? My own lack of resolution, my feelings seem to be begging to be noticed. Instead of looking for someone else, why don't I begin giving the child within me what I always wanted for myself? There seems to be a child inside of me, conceived many years ago, just waiting for his rediscovery. Why not begin looking at my world and then create a new one which is safe enough for feeling and trusting, a world that is safe enough for dreams?

Commitment

The decision to stop running from my child involves a major commitment. Every way of life despite how unsatisfying it may have been has still been the path of my life. Letting go of my old ways and beginning a new path, this one closer to my heart, is dependent upon how much I value myself.

Initially, anyone who considers having a baby weighs carefully the burden of supporting that baby and always being there for that child, versus the love and joy it will bring to the world. The decision to give rebirth to the forgotten child within me demands equal responsibility if he is going to be cared for and nurtured as he deserves. Financial, social, and personal obligations of all kinds have to be looked at in order for my child to have his deserved priority. As with other children, I do not want to raise my child to make up for the lack of love in my world. I want to make room for my child to become himself.

Originally my childhood, my feelings, became confused and controlled by other people's needs and expectations. Now the only person my child is responsible to, the only person who can make excuses for not loving and caring for who he is, is myself.

In the past I lived on the assumption that I was not in control of my life. My parents and other people were given the authority to determine my life. Making the commitment to raise my child in the world means beginning to realize that I am either controlling or giving up control over my life. Now I am the parent and trusting teacher my child looks to while coming into his own. It is up to me to either turn my head or listen to his needs, my feelings and begin acting on what I want. Realizing the child within me can be nothing less than creating the path of my second childhood and protecting it until my child can take care of himself.

Environment

There are teachers who will teach me how to think, therapists who will help me relearn to feel. But my greatest allies are those who support me in relearning how to trust, and be with my most desired path. Each moment relearning to trust my experience is another moment closer to the feeling child I brought into the world. The people who want me to be one place or another where they have found their hearts, love me the most when they encourage me to pursue my own necessary way.

Finding the path of my heart initially means changing the adult life which is limiting my child. This means giving up all the habits as an adult which deny my feelings. For example, cigarette smoking, overeating, oversleeping, drugs, alcohol, behavior which tries to make me feel bigger or different than I really am, all helps deny my child. This includes relationships which make me feel bad and relationships which make me have no feelings at all. Once I know my child, my feelings, the teacher within will know how much room my child needs in my life. Meanwhile the activities I do which more or less only relieve tension, which experience little or no feelings, are the things I want to change to develop the path of my heart.

I begin by creating safe environments for me to have my feelings. This may be my own room, a certain part of a playground, an open and friendly restaurant, a friend's basement, an isolated mountain valley. People and places which encourage me to be as I want, give my child safety in order to risk coming out again in the world. Gradually I will accumulate more and more special places and persons, a life where I will feel free enough to be with my child, being who I am.

My child will not come out all at once. No matter how much time I set aside and how safe a place I provide, he has been forgotten, controlled, and in general unloved too long to suddenly appear. I am too accustomed to a life of adult

Some teachers insist learning to think is the way.
Some therapists insist learning to feel is the way.

The people who support me in learning to trust
First my heart, then my head and child,
My will to think and feel as I want,
Are my greatest allies.

struggle and surrender to just have a feeling child appear in the world. Giving my feelings a half hour a day or an entire Saturday afternoon to be as they want, no excuses, may be the beginning. Unless I have something to occupy this time, I may not know what to do. But that is a good sign. Now is the time for not being always busy, always planning activities with my busy adult mind. This is the time for my child, planning my experience from the point of view of my feelings. In most every adult is a four year old who is hurting, a five year old who likes toy stores, a ten year old who misses his mother, and who likes hiking with a friend. Perhaps there is a sixteen year old who is interested in sex but is shy and timid. The experience of the child within is infinite, buried and waiting to be loved. My child is waiting to continue growing once I provide the environment where he feels safe enough to do so.

Feeling

As I let go of my old path including the adult habits that deny my feelings, I begin to feel the tension behind or beneath them. For example, instead of smoking or overeating I begin to feel my lungs and stomach and the feelings needing attention and love. Instead of avoiding my fantasies and desires, I may begin to feel the anger suppressed in my muscles from always denying myself. Sometimes I may not have reasons for my feelings. Other times I may react to seemingly insignificant events happening to me. I do not need reasons to be with my child. These are symbolic times where my child is literally coming back into the world. He deserves my allowance for his periods of overreaction, sensitivity, and need. My head instead of thinking of others is relearning how to think for my child. I want to provide for and love my unfolding experience. In many ways I am like a pregnant mother trying to give as natural and loving birth to my child as I can. I want to be sensitive to his needs and desires.

Support

There are people who can think and cannot feel. Other people have so much feeling they cannot think clearly. Doctors call some of the former, "neurotics" and the latter, "psychotics." But the labels are less important than the needs of the child within each. The child is either buried somewhere or is naked and alone, screaming in the darkness. Children need to be picked up and loved. Each child has his own needs, his own ways to be cared for, and they are always changing. Instead of always looking to my head or someone else's for the answers, I look to my child, learning to trust my feelings and thoughts for the way.

Some people may want extra help. Sometimes in the path of my second childhood I need someone who is not frightened by my feelings or unclear thinking. I need to be able to feel safe in order to let go of my head controlling my feelings and just let my child feel, scream, kick, and holler. At times loving my child is allowing myself to have a temper tantrum, a temper tantrum I was not allowed to have sometime in the past. I cannot be real with my child with someone who does not accept his own, especially when I am not sure of him myself. Similarly I can't allow my mind to be crazy with someone who does not accept their own periods of temporary craziness. I want to be with someone who will not feel a need to push or pull me but will love me, trusting me to find my own necessary way. This may be a lover, a therapist, a teacher but most of all this person will be a friend. We may make a contract, an agreement with one another, to give support to each other's child while we are learning to take care of each ourselves. The safety in our relationship is most important. Even more important is the safety I give myself not to control, hurt, or limit my emerging child.

Needs

My child needs to cry and scream, letting the knots of tension in his stomach go. He wants lots of toys and crayons to express his feelings. My child wants a stuffed elephant. Peo-

18

ple who feel good to my child are fun to play with. My child wants me to tell him that I love him and care about him when he is tired and sad. He may want to go to the park, take a bubble bath, and eat french fries every day for an entire week. Now is the time when I am either going to have a loving relationship with my child or he is going to feel uncared for as he has in the past. Like other children my child needs presents, special trips, and to feel I love him especially when he is unhappy and feels hopeless. All of his confusion, hurt and pain is coming to the surface. My child cannot grow all alone. He needs others but most of all my child needs me.

I cannot really picture myself
With too big of a heart.
There seems to be no end to trusting
My thoughts and feelings.

I have yet to hear of anyone
Suffering from too much love.

My Choices

The rebirth of my child is painful in the beginning. I have not been avoiding him for so many years without reason. I have been frightened that he would be overwhelming. I have not felt safe enough to feel him so I have tried to forget him instead. Now that he is finally out, he is angry about being locked up for so long. I do not blame him. He is hurt from all the times he was not loved. He is wanting to be held and be happy.

The important thing for me to remember is that now I am responsible for my child. Now I am in control and have choices to take care of his feelings.

When starting my second childhood I will naturally re-create my first childhood, my old painful ways unless I continually remind myself of an alternative. My second childhood is learning that I always have an alternative. In the beginning I just stopped the adult habits that prevented me from feeling. Now that I have my feelings I will automatically go back to old patterns of behaving, patterns which were not satisfying but nevertheless were well known and followed out of routine. I will set up my old struggles, the life of compromise and surrender which smothered my child before. I will give up the controls, my power as I did before unless I remind my feelings that they are mine, my child that he belongs to me. I can live in the pain of my old world, my first childhood, forever unless I provide him with new choices.

Even once firmly set upon the new path, echoes from my past urge me to forget my child again and again. More than likely my first childhood will be repeated unless I spend extra effort loving my child so he does not stay with his painful ways. I may give the people around me the controls to my feelings time and again until I learn that I am in control, I am my own director. My path now is taking back the power I give to others to control and define my life so that I can use it to create a new way.

The closer I am to my child, the safer my environment, the more choices I will know to give my feelings resolution. When I am stuck in one experience over and over, I am not feeling safe enough and loved enough to move on. I do not believe I deserve anything more. Children, besides having their basic needs met, need to be touched and to feel secure. Children need honesty and to know what's expected of them. My child is no exception.

Giving my child the way of his heart means loving him in ways he typically was never loved. Sometimes I may literally feel like a little baby, looking like one also. Initially I may just want to cry, breathing deeply, experiencing more and more of my lost self. But no baby wants to cry forever.

My baby wants to be picked up and held. My baby wants to be told that everything is all right and that I will take care of him. Loving and caring for him, he begins to understand he has choices, his second childhood is not simply more of his past in a new setting. Gradually interacting, playing and trusting my child, I am assuming control over my experience. The world does not have the power to determine my feelings. I am becoming self determined. Every tear, every smile is releasing more of my body back to feeling. Feeling my child recovered, my body is back to a more fully breathing, alive state. The child buried within me gradually becomes less and less of a mass of tension and more and more of a conscious, moving spirit. Developing my choices gives me access to my child. I can be twenty five, eighteen, ten, five, or two. Similarly I have more access to my body. Feeling and trusting myself I feel and trust my body.

I Deserve

Whenever I am overwhelmed and feeling hopeless, my child is crying for attention, crying to know he deserves better. As an adult I never get overwhelmed, feeling hopeless and helpless, because I always have choices to take care of myself. The part of me which does become overwhelmed is my child, who actually did not experience choices to get his needs met and became hopeless and helpless instead. As an actual infant I was not powerful and independent. If others did not meet my needs I was left simply needing. I did not know I deserved anything more. I learned ways of trying to please others hoping they would give me what I wanted. Now I want to learn ways to please myself, hoping I will learn that I can care for my own needing child. Now when my needs appear as gigantic and impossible to take care of, I know I am seeing the world from my old childhood eyes. My child is waiting for me to tell him that he deserves an alternative.

In the past I would probably have worked extra hard, maybe get sick, eat more and more, manipulate and appeal to my friends, being desperate to feel accepted and get the love I wanted. But no matter what road I took as an adult,

21

my child was left needing. Something was missing. I was taking care of myself as if I was only an adult forgetting that there is also a two year old, nine year old, and sixteen year old needing inside of me. No wonder working harder, over-eating or sleeping, some new book or teacher to believe in, a love note from a friend was never completely satisfying. What nine year old feels better working harder? What sixteen year old wants a new book or teacher to believe in? What child wants a love note? Children want to be hugged, played with, and made to feel they deserve more. Learning what I really want, then responding to my desires, unfolds the path to my garden. Telling my child he deserves to be respected, loved, and trusted is the path to my heart. My adult ways of compromise, struggle, and surrender began long ago. When I started to feel I did not have any choice, that I did not deserve anything more, I began to accept a life that was different than I wanted. What child freely chooses to surrender himself? What child naturally chooses to fill his life full of struggle? Knowing that I did not have choices and currently do, reminds me that I have alternatives for a new way. My adult energy which has been invested in denying my feelings and desires is now free to create a path with my heart. My natural child, a person who does not want to struggle and compromise himself, deserves to return to his garden.

Cosmic Excuses

Excuses, excuses are the heroes of the adult world of painful struggle. As a child I slowly began to accept all the excuses given to me explaining why I could not be who I wanted to be. I accepted the right of others to determine my being. With the dependence upon the world for my welfare, I had lots of reason to gradually accept all the excuses given to me for becoming compromised.

Now once again I am full of excuses for not loving my child, for not caring for my feelings. The major difference however is when I was little I was given excuses by others, who actually did have power over my being. Now the excuses come first and foremost from myself. Sometimes I am the last person to be my own friend. I try to give my environment, my boss, my girlfriend, my past and countless other excuses as reasons for not being who I want, for not caring for my desires. My boss will not accept me if I show my feelings. My girlfriend is scared of my true desires. I do not want to lose this job, this relationship, this friend. The potential excuses I have to struggle and surrender myself are endless. Sometimes I continue my excuses for so long that even my boss or girlfriend says for me to stop punishing myself. Sometimes I am the last person to come to the aid of my feelings. This does not make my child feel very loved and hopeful.

The truth is I don't believe I deserve a job where I can show my feelings or I would be working there. I don't believe I deserve to have a girlfriend to share my fantasies or I would have one. Admitting I want to be compromised, that I believe I deserve nothing more, is the beginning of gaining control over my life. Recognizing that a greater part of myself enjoys a compromised situation than another part wants to risk changing it, is the beginning of being able to respond to more of myself and be responsible. It is all right to enjoy feeling surrendered, to enjoy pain. If I did not enjoy it, why would I be there? It is the path I believe I deserve and am accustomed to. If I did not enjoy struggling why am I struggling, unless it is the usual way for me to experience myself?

This may sound crazy
But sometimes
I have hundreds of excuses
Not to feel good.

As an adult I repeat setting up my life in painful situations, maintain myself compromised and struggling because this is what I learned as a child. Until I know I deserve an alternative and feel safe enough to try it, I will enjoy my pain as the path to trying to get the love and security I need.

The first cosmic excuse is I HAVE NO CHOICE. Believing I have no choices makes it so much easier to live my life surrendered and enjoy it. As soon as I am aware I have choices, suddenly my excuses for suffering no longer hold. Unless I confess I need to feel pain right now, I have no recourse but to follow a more pleasurable way.

My second cosmic excuse, which is sometimes greater than the first is MY ALTERNATIVES ARE ONLY WORSE THAN WHAT I HAVE ALREADY. If I cannot have NO CHOICES, I'll create a choice which is far worse than the current one which makes my compromised place not so painful. The most common examples are "I cannot leave this job because I will not find another, I cannot leave this relationship because there is no other." I cannot change these hopeless feelings because I know of no others. Suffering, I believe I deserve nothing better. I continue to hope that the world will somehow change and take care of me. My child, my heart, and my head are all given away, surrendered out of control. My hopeless child remains helpless until I love him, remind him that my head, heart, and child are inside of me instead of others.

What child naturally enjoys pain? Giving up pain as a way of life begins by admitting I am choosing it, proceeding to love and care for my hurting child. He needs to know he

Believing I am drowning
I become convinced that I have no choices.
It is so much easier to feel bad
When I think there is nothing I can do.

deserves so much better. Whenever I believe I have no choices or only choices which are worse than my current situation, I am seeing the world from my old child's point of view. Now as an adult I always have choices, I know I deserve better. The world is no longer controlling me unless I allow it to do so. Every time I take care of my child in pain, he becomes stronger, more trusting, gradually knowing his path the way he wants it. The times I am feeling most overwhelmed are the times my child most deserves to be loved. I have the choices to create or deny his resolution.

The Result

Changing my life's path, raising my child, I am becoming free to experience my whole self. Instead of the world telling me what's inside of me I am learning to express myself from the inside outward. My internal experience is cared for, nurtured, and defended. My days are planned from the most selfish, hungry parts of myself. Life is no longer struggling, wishing to fly away from itself. Each morning is an opportunity to remember my dreams and plan my way from my heart.

Learning to love and accept love from others begins when I learn to love my own feelings. When I care about my own child, I can believe somebody else does also. Learning to love my child, my unresolved nature, I trust living my own will. The door is always through my heart. When looking everywhere but in my heart seems easiest, I know that is when I most need myself. I begin by giving to my need. In every conflict, first I give myself permission for being there. Telling my child it is all right to be in conflict, to be in pain, begins the resolution of finding my choices. Realizing my choices, I follow my heart to my child, trusting my feelings as to which choice to follow. Becoming responsible for my conflicts, being able to respond, I am freer.

Each conflict resolved I feel a little stronger, trust my way a little more, know I deserve still better. Each conflict is resolved with love. Accumulating resolution is as accumulating love. Love unfolds the path of my greatest will.

Meditation
For Me Is Being As Outrageously Myself As I Possibly Can

Years of meditation
Has not emptied my head
Or silenced my feelings
As in the Eastern tradition.

But has exploded my heart
With me laughing more
And loving
Pursuing my own will!

On Being Jealous, Angry, Possessive and Other Forms of Meditation

Screaming, crying, running through the park, playing, enjoying sex, sitting and quietly breathing — I am always meditating. The more I enjoy myself breathing in all my experiences, the more successful my meditation. The more serious and tense I am, the poorer my meditation unless I want to be serious and tense. In that case I may be quite clear being as serious and tense as I wish. Meditation for me is being as outrageously myself as I can possibly be. Years of meditation has not emptied my head or silenced my feelings as in the Eastern tradition but has exploded my heart with me laughing more and loving pursuing my own will.

When I want to seriously make my life more together, my meditation more clear, I think of all the ways I am denying my child, my feelings. Usually the part of me which I am most often avoiding is the jealous, angry, possessive, hungry little monster inside of me. I can sit quietly and breathe in and out, in and out and try to believe he is not there. But sooner or later, and I hope sooner, he creeps out or explodes out of me demanding attention. There is this child inside of me who just won't sit still. He wants and wants and wants and wants and wants some more. When someone else is enjoying himself, he is jealous. When his day is going bad, he is angry. And when he is happy, he wants to hold onto everything in his world and is absolutely unwilling to share, at least for the moment. The more I try to be cool and deny my child, the more he twists and turns, squirming into a little monster.

He becomes spiteful, aggressive, sullen, violent, or withdrawn. Sometimes he could break about everything in the house or break his arm to spite everyone including himself. Other times he just runs havoc around and around in my stomach giving me an ulcer, the flu, or hunger pains until I thoroughly stuff him down with food and still don't feel at all satisfied. One way or another my child will jump up and down until I somehow relieve the tension and tire him out, or choose to take care of him.

My child is always reminding me of the love and attention he needs. Sometimes through sex, the more desperate he feels, the more he dances and teases me in my groin. When I am climbing up the walls for a sexual partner, my child is pounding the same walls to make some contact with me. He is sick and tired of being ignored and demands some attention. My child is willing to make me miserable physically, sexually, emotionally, socially—anyway he can until I will finally take care of him. The longer I try to forget this child, the more unmanagable he is when he finally surfaces. This I know from lots of experience.

Once I was involved in a love affair. I couldn't tell my girlfriend how jealous, angry, and possessive I was of her when I felt her other relationships received more attention than ours. I was afraid of losing her until I found out I may lose my child instead. While being understanding of her not being with me, my child would be awake all night, tossing and turning, screaming and pounding, hurting and crying in my sleep. This continued until my child let me know that I had the choice to either understand her or understand him. The more difficult the choice became, the more angry and hurt he was. Finally beginning to recognize him, both my girlfriend and my child began to respect me more. I began to trust myself more and my meditation became much clearer.

My meditation reached one of its highest states when we were fighting, screaming at one another how we felt and

Some people meditate with their eyes closed
Chanting a mantra, being different than they are
But I meditate with my eyes open
Because it All is Right here.

The only certain words, breathing, or exercise necessary
Seems to be the words, breath, or exercise I'm currently doing.
My meditation is as revealing
As I am Right Now.

As I am Right Now
Is the most complete meditation
I know
Right Now . . .

what we wanted from the other. My jealous, angry, and possessive feelings gave my child greater control over my life. Upon setting a safe environment where the relationship itself would not be questioned, her child as well became as demanding and assuming as mine. The more we allowed the child in each of us to stand firmly upon their heals, shouting how they felt, demanding what they wanted, the firmer and more complete we each felt. More important than winning was just fighting, meditating. Finally with my sweat all over me, exhausted and my friend feeling the same, we declared our meditation together as a success, both of us fighting for our child the best we could

Meditation doesn't always take such vigorous forms but keeping on the look out for the desires of my child helps prevent developing an angry monster later on to contend with. I may not always be able to meet his desires. But my child, like children in general, wants to know that it is all right to want and that he deserves to have his wishes come true. Admitting my jealous, angry, and possessive nature, telling my child that I understand and care about his feelings saves my life and his from lots of misery. Expressing my jealousy, anger, and possessiveness whenever it is safe to do so is the most special way I can tell my child that I love him.

If I cannot directly express my child, finding some other way to take care of my feelings is partly what meditation is all about. Developing choices, lots of choices to substitute for the ways I deny my feelings develops the strongest path of my heart. Being open, breathing deeply, meditation is listening to my child moment by moment. Continually listening and giving to my child, I learn what I really want. My child assumes more and more control over my day and the easier it is for me to respond to him. I am not talking about being a permissive parent, having an overly permissive childhood. My child wants to be loved and this includes giving him safety, structure, guiding him upon his opening way. The more my child is unleashed, the more all the shakeups in my world are understood and the less often they occur.

For some reason many people believe that meditation

means avoiding falling in love, learning not to feel jealous, angry, and possessive. But for me falling in love is the closest I can be with my child, my true nature. Allowing my child to feel close to the world is the most affirming experience I can have. The more I fall in love, the happier my child. Meditation is just learning how to be nice to all of my feelings in the process. I may fall in love several times in a few days. Feeling friends, toys, beautiful sunsets, every moment I risk feeling close to, is affirming to my child. Meditation is often the path of my greatest risk, coming, coming closer until I am actually touching the moment. The more I touch my child, my feelings, the freer I am in my day approaching what I want, the more powerful and centered I feel.

Upon successfully learning to meditate, feeling jealous, angry, and possessive is not so difficult to do. The easier it is for me to accept my jealous, angry, and possessive child, the easier it is for me to risk falling in love. Sometimes that's all I seem to be doing is falling in love again, again, and again. The more I meditate, the more I am in love. I'm afraid if I take my meditation too seriously I will fall hopelessly in love forever. Breathing, feeling, listening, meditation is learning how to love my child. Learning how to love my child is learning how to love the world. When I am loving the world, my child is the happiest.

Loving
My
Addictions

Life's meaning seems to be searched for everywhere but where it already is. New therapies and books, Gurus and journeys of all kinds are consumed in the meanwhile. Studies of primitive societies, apes and monkeys currently spotlight the search for life's nakedness and truth. Politics, art, drugs, sex are all alternate routes. But if I want to find the most naked moments which hold some truth over my being, I need to look no further than my moments of being out of control. The compulsive or desperate moments controlling my experience are where I have given up my freedom and set limits to my being. Just beneath my compulsive rituals or addictive behavior I find myself, my child most naked.

My inclinations to smoke or drink, compulsively think or perform some behavior always continue until I feel safe enough to make another choice. Just beneath my addictions is my child, feeling so naked and vulnerable, so out of control that he feels frozen, unable to feel. In every desperate movement I realize the sometimes raw truth that I am the creator of my experience or controlled by other forces. I point in all directions trying to give proper aim to my problem until I feel my child running havoc over my heart and mind. My addictions express the split between my child and head, my feelings and thoughts. Loving my addictions facilitates their marriage, developing my heart, my will.

33

Compulsively eating, sleeping, taking drugs, working, or acting out a particular sexual fantasy, every part of my day which feels driven is my child taking over my life expressing his needs. Some addictions are more socially acceptable than others. Some are more taken for granted or unnoticed. Many feel predetermined, undetermined, anything but self-determined. Within every grasp for a fix whether it be a syringe, a lover, a drink, an order controlling someone else or a piece of cake—within that grasp lies the admission of being out of control and the opportunity to assume responsibility for my needing child. It is within the moments of being out of control that the knife of my will experiences its edges. My addictions express my most basic truths.

In many ways, addictions are defenses against living more fully. We abuse ourselves with the food and drugs we consume as well as with the technology, environment, and government we live with. There are hundreds of ways we as people and as a society are out of control. Authority can hardly be responsible, able to respond without thinking, trusting, and feeling. Our society can have a head, heart, and child only inasmuch as people, we trust the head, heart and child within each of us. I am not out of control when my head cares for my child, trusting my own will.

Believing that cigarette smoking, alcohol, being socially withdrawn or hyperactive, believing that my behavior has control over me, eliminates any opportunity for choosing my way and being more fully self determined. The problem is not the addiction but being unable to more fully choose and determine my life. Addictions, as all defenses against living more fully, may be unnecessary. But, if parts of my life are out of control, denying or changing those parts will not satisfy me until the needs of my child are satisfied. The parts of my life that are out of control are my openings to discovering and nurturing my second childhood.

I am acting out my child's compulsive or desperate feelings because he is not feeling safe enough to make any other choice. Trying to just stop or change my addictions is telling my child which parts of him are all right and which must be forgotten. At these moments my child wants to be seen for who he is and loved. Being controlled at this vulnerable point only further weakens my failing will. Now I need trust to begin trusting my feelings once again. Loving my child, realizing why he has chosen this addiction, defense, resistance to living more fully, he begins to feel safer, to feel his feelings, taking care of them, instead of denying them, running away, or trying to change them. All addictions by their nature express a fear of being a child, a fear of feeling. Loving my addictions, I am caring for the fear I have of my own feelings. It is always fear that holds my heart captive. The closer I am to knowing and loving my fear, the closer I am to freeing my will. My addictions contain the opening to my fears which hold the means to my heart.

When I am feeling compulsive, my child is needing my recognition of who he is, out of control. He is feeling threatened. His pain is hiding, desperate for a loving environment which expresses the message he is worth loving. There are lots of techniques or exercises he can go to where

I am running scared.
All of my compulsive or desperate moments
Are covering my FEAR
Of feeling, feeling my child.

Loving my addictions,
Giving safety to my FEAR,
Remembering no one is controlling my child but me
Frees my heart, strengthens my will!

someone will make him feel better. But that is my problem. At this moment my child is feeling my utter hopelessness to create my own way. I feel him grasping for just about anything which will change his feelings. Sometimes I just sit and listen to his anger and frustration. I remember that no one is controlling how he feels right now but me. My child is running, jumping to do something, not just sit. I could get up, do something, and take away his feelings. Or I can sit with him, waiting for his restlessness to settle into his own necessary action. I close my eyes and listen to his rumblings. I hold him, letting my arms and legs go the way they want to go. I take his hand and run it across my face. Touching, sitting, breathing, the feelings boil out of me. My child starts screaming, pounding, crying, or smiling his relief. Giving my child choices to come to his own course whatever that might be is his way of resolution. My child's resolution frees me.

Taking away the fix or giving a fix to an addict is far less important than having an environment which further threatens an addict's child or gives his child warmth and security. My child does not stop screaming until he is listened to and cared for. Sometimes the only way he can scream is through some compulsive or desperate action. Listening for and caring for these acts, lessens the need for my child to escalate his desperation. My child as most children needs my attention, to be held and know he is all right. Loving my fear frees my heart to feeling and thinking once again. Fear versus safety distinguishes the course of my resolution.

My world, including my addictions can feel as hard and unchanging as concrete or as flexible and easy as blinking my eyes. My world including my addictions is but an hallucination of my will. I can spend time trying to control or somehow change my hallucination. Or I can center my life upon freeing my will. The weaker my will, the stronger the hallucination. The stronger my will, the more I am in control, being the creator of my world. My addictions, my needs and pains are but hallucinations created by my failing will. The more directly, I focus my energy upon my will, the less control the hallucinations have over me. I am hallucinating because my feelings are overwhelming. Giving my complex adult life of hallucinations safety to feel, the simplicity of being a child unfolds.

As much as my experience is as concrete, unchangeable, lays the potential for a simple action like blinking to remind me I am able to create a beautiful experience. It is all a matter of taking a second look, instead of trying to change, I create, unleashing my will. Upon opening my eyes I feel stuck or free, at one with the moment, all depending upon my self acceptance and love. Loving my addictions for me has become a process of learning how to blink. Taking another look, letting go of my will, frees my experience. Blinking, I am focusing my world. Blinking and breathing, closing my eyes and inhaling at the same time, opening my eyes and exhaling, I am creating the world. The heaviness or subtlety of my experience, creating or being out of control, are ultimately for me to determine.

Realizing over and over I am the source and creator of my experience is the opening way. The times of greatest desperation or of emptiness, feeling nothingness, are the times when my child is most frightened of being who he wants to be. The conflicts I am experiencing are but symbols of my will compromising, adjusting, exploding, panicking, blooming into my own. My compulsions express symbolicly what my child really wants. Being addicted by definition means to be without self control. My child is feeling too unsafe to feel out of control so I am symbolicly acting out my feelings through my behavior. Instead of looking for my usual escapes or means to relieve my tension, I can begin relieving the burden of my child, who is hurting and trying to be an adult in control at the same time. When he feels safe enough he will burst crying and screaming freeing himself from his overwhelming feelings. Sometimes it is ok, in fact necessary, for me to not be in control and let my child go, having a temper tantrum if he may. Within my adult searching for something new is always my child hoping, expecting I will tune into him and my unfolding garden. All the flowers lie within if I have the courage and support to weather the storm.

Nurturing my garden is dependent upon my nurturing my will. Realizing my conflicts are a creation of my unfolding will places me in the center of my world. The problems and pain in my life are but hallucinations, illusions that I am finding real. These illusions continue their grasp over me until I recognize all my excuses to not care for my child, trusting my child and head to flow my necessary way. Each feeling cared for, the great weight, my hallucination, is let go of. The weight of the world in general is realized for its illusory qualities. Beneath the hallucination, my garden is always waiting for me. My child is as far away as a gigantic struggle or as blinking. My will is as far away as my heart. Without my fear, the hallucinations I believe in, the illusions I give my life to , do not exist. My world is but my will experiencing itself.

Listening
to
My Body

As I come closer to my child I am realizing my desire to listen to my body. When my feelings are too great for me to experience, my body begins to show signs of those feelings. I can get headaches, stomach and back aches, a sore arm or mouth. Sometimes my whole body collapses with a fever as a part of me seems to shake and boil out of me. When I feel fat, my child feels stuffed down and pushed out of the way. When I feel too skinny, my child feels overexposed. My child is always talking to me through my experience of my body. It is up to me to choose to respond to him or ignore him. When I am in pain it is my choice to see the pain as part of a healing and cleansing process or a process of getting sick and coming apart.

When my child is fed up, needing something from me, one sure way to get my attention is by attacking my body. When he attacks, by learning to listen to and for him, I begin seeing it is no coincidence that today I have a headache or today I am sick with the flu. If I have been ignoring signs or lack of signs (lack of feeling in my body) more serious ailments often occur. If I have hurt my knee and I am limping, my child is telling me he's feeling crippled and wants me to know it. A pounding headache and my child is telling me quite directly that he's been pounding to get to me. If I have a sore back, sure enough my child is telling me he's feeling the whole world on his back and wants a rest. What my pains mean for me may be different than what they mean for someone else. Regardless, I can find meaning and take care of my experience or deny parts of myself which are expressing themselves.

Many people believe their emotional and physical pains are uncontrollable. They believe the problems in their lives are coincidental or by accident. Many are looking everywhere but in their own conflicts for their healing resolution. By declaring my pain as uncontrollable I know I am refusing to listen to my child. Attempting to deny all responsibility for being sick, I am denying my ability to respond and recognize the healing process taking place.

I don't understand why there are physical doctors, psychiatric, social and spiritual doctors as well. I am but one person. When my body is in pain, my physical, emotional, social, spiritual self is not in balance. The problems surfacing in my life are part of all of me, my child, my unresolved experience, assuming itself, asking to be taken care of. My child, my unresolved experience may surface with a physical or a social conflict. But it is my child that needs my attention for my life is out of order.

Certainly whether it is a physical or emotional pain, social or spiritual problem I can go to a doctor and have his head, his meaning, take over for my own and relieve my symptoms. Or I can seek guidance realizing my pains are only symptoms of something greater in my life being off center. Doctors can be an excuse to deny responsibility for my pain or help in gaining control over my experience. Doctors can declare I am sick and treat me. Or doctors can help me recognize the healing process taking place which my discomfort is demonstrating. Ultimately nobody heals me against my own will. A shot does not heal me. A shot helps me build my body, strengthening me so I can heal myself. I can seek help as a way to deny my need to give to myself. Or I can seek help revitalizing my own healing powers, to heal myself. The most famous surgeon in the world doesn't heal anyone but helps people to heal themselves.

My doctor is first and foremost a wise voice inside of me who knows my child. When I am in pain, I do not try to deny it or run from it but listen to my body talking to me. Through the course of trusting my child to express himself, my head, my wise doctor begins developing the path of my natural health. If my heart trusts my head, my thoughts will provide the best prescription for my child. My pain means a lack of care for my child and my head, relating to one another. But most of all my pain means a lack of trust that my heart has the will to provide for me. The healing process always involves for me developing my heart, so I trust being in control, my will flowing once again.

When I am in difficulty I often relax my body and my child and then seek the wise man in my head. After my body is calmed, I literally search out and picture a wise man in my consciousness. Upon finding him, I ask him questions towards my resolution. As it would take me time to recognize my child, learning about and respecting the wise man in my head follows a similar process. In either process my heart is the central door. In one I am learning to trust my feelings, the other to trust my intuition. As I have been taught that the answers for my feelings are everywhere in the world but trusting my own child, I have been taught that the answers for my head are everywhere in the world but trusting my own intuition.

In little ways everyday I eat what I think is right, go where it feels right, and I am with who I want to be with. Developing my ability to listen to my wise man only strengthens my control and ability to respond to the world. Whenever I feel in a rush for something or someone to rescue my child or my head, now is the opportunity to trust my feelings and thoughts to care for myself. Somewhere in my heart is always the resolution to my pain.

Sometimes the wise man in my head may actually suggest that I go to a doctor for help and guidance. When I do not trust my wise man to provide me with the full prescription, he may suggest my going to a doctor to get in touch with my choices. The wise man insists however that I go to a doctor that knows that he cannot heal me but help me to heal

My doctor is the wise man inside of me
If my heart trusts my head.
My intuition will provide the best prescription
For my needing child.

myself. This doctor may absolutely know the right course
for me to take. But instead of controlling me, my child, he
trusts me to arrive at my own resolution with his guidance of
helping me develop my choices. This doctor instead of becoming my head and doing my thinking for me, loves me to
trust my heart and my own healing processes. He knows the
latest techniques or the newest medicine is not the answer.
He knows that modern psychiatry and medicine have found
cures for many pains, many symptoms and ailments but they
don't know the reasons for our problems. Only I can find the
meaning and resolution to *my* experience. The pains surfacing in my life are for me to ultimately respond to as parts of
myself shouting, crying, begging, asking the rest of me to
know what I am feeling. The pills and machines used in my
healing process are only aids in strengthening my own will,
trusting my heart to provide the way.

When I am physically disabled my child is telling me
how he is denied. My crippled self is literally surfacing. I am
as I appear to be. When I am sick, I get well by being sick and
loving my healing self to health. When I am well, I appear

42

well. Instead of expecting something or someone else to take care of me, I expect things and others to aid my failing will. Some of my pains are indicators of current stress I'm feeling in relationships or while working. Some of my pains are old unresolved past experiences still surfacing in my life. Whether physical or emotional pain, my body is talking to me. Learning how to trust my head while listening to my child, I find my resolution. The more I know and love my child, the more I know and love my wise man to take care of him. From listening and trusting him in the past, it is easier for me to follow his way now in the present.

When my feeling child is uncared for, my physical self will let me know. When my body is ignored, my feelings will tell me. My body is my vehicle for my experience. Anything malfunctioning in my body controls or limits my experience of the world. Listening, caring, I am realizing more and more I am not separate from the world. I am the food I eat, the people I'm with, the environment I am a part of. I am my experience. Treating my body is treating my whole world. Somewhere my diet is off balance, correcting itself. I want to get in touch with the adjusting taking place, my changing appetite. Somewhere I am not getting enough of the right kinds of food whether it is vegetables, sun, parks, friends. Somewhere my need for love is not being met and I am having trouble trusting my own will. My needing child is always expressing itself through my body. What other choices does he have to show his needs for attention? Recognizing my child I am continually learning the way of my heart, my changing appetite of life.

With physical pain as with any kind of pain, it is my chosen experience which determines my affirming course. I can be a victim, out of control or I can give myself permission and begin nurturing my child, heart, and head, assuming responsibility for my needing self. Perhaps I do not choose the events, the accidents in my life. But I do choose my experience and reactions to those events. Pain by definition is a lack of love. Pain is the vehicle to my heart. I am always trusting my way to a better world. The child and wise man within me are simply waiting for my acceptance.

43

The world stands between me and my child.
I can struggle with my parents, friends, teachers
Forever until I realize my child is the one
I am not accepting.

My child often believes
The world has to accept him
Before I can recognize him
And give him the love he deserves.

Letting the world stand between
Me and my feelings
I am forever separated from my child
Being on opposite sides of the world can be quite lonely!

Revealing Myself Through the Circle of Fear

Inside, my heart is always pumping. Pain, sickness and other obstacles rarely stop my heart from continuing its regular flow. Indeed the constant pulse seems to heal any obstruction. My heart is the center of my body's action. Outside, with my feeling and social life, my heart is always beating too. However sometimes my will seems to stop and dry up with even a thought of pursuing its way. Imagine if my heart literally stopped and questioned itself as my will does in pursuit of its day? Until my will flows as automatically as my heart, pumping steadily in adversity as well as peace, I know I am not at the center of my life's action. When I no longer believe the world has a grasp over my life, my will, and my heart will be together, beating strongly.

At some early age when I was very vulnerable, I must have become so frightened that my will momentarily stopped beating. Attacks of will caused a hesitant and sometimes sporadic pulse. Even as an adult some fearful memories must still be preventing my will from its steady beat. Until I feel through this fear, until I love away this hold on my heart, my will experiences a circle of fear about me. Ordinary events and relationships appear as enormous and overwhelming to a heart whose will was stopped and controlled at a very early age. Beginning as a small infant a circle of fear

45

has separated me from my heart. Everything standing between me and my will stands between me and my heart coming together, beating strongly. As I reveal myself to the world I am revealing my will to my heart. As I am separated from the world I feel, my will is separated from its pumping source.

Understanding myself through this circle of fear is no easy task. Returning my will to my heart from wherever it may have strayed involves assuming responsibility for my will just as my heart responds to my body. When my body needs more blood I provide it. My will must provide more attention when my world demands it. I am always affirming my will's right to pump my life's flow. It is as silly to believe the world has claim to my will as it is to think somebody else can control my heartbeat.

When I am struggling for a pay raise, for my girlfriend to love me, for the political candidate of my choice, my heart and will are struggling to be back together. It seems no surprise that no matter how much money I have, how much my girlfriend demonstrates her love for me, or whoever is elected—I am not satisfied. Until my child resolves the fear that panics my will, my heart and will are out of harmony. Until I love my frightened child, my adult life will be lacking my full strength and desire. As long as my will remains crippled, my adult and my child will be separated. The world will be a stage for repeated struggle and compromise until my heart and will establish a mutual trust and flow. In the process I can place changing my job, friends, political candidates between me and my child, or I can create a new world, safe enough for me to be responsive to my wishes. This is not to say that I do not have employers, friends, and support political candidates. Only I don't drag my child out into the world in search for my heart. It is so much easier to search for my heart where it really is, inside of me. Revealing myself to the world, I remember I am revealing my child to my heart. As difficult as it seems for the world to accept me, it is for my heart to love my child as he really is. Whenever I am shaking with fear of someone else's rejection, my child is overwhelmed and frightened, my heart will no longer provide for him. When my child feels safe and loved by me, the world's reaction to me one way or another has little weight. I am taking care of my feelings, creating my choices, pursuing my own way.

In the beginning I was cared for. Provided with protection and warmth, I adjusted to my environment's needs and expectations. When I was under the control of others, they also assumed responsibility for me. With time however it became expected that I take more and more care of myself, become responsible for my choices. Gradually as an adult I found myself responsible for my life but unsure who or what to respond to. I have been responding to others for so long that I couldn't suddenly identify me separate from the world I lived in. My second childhood has been a process of learning what I want and assuming control over my life.

I am coming closer and closer to the course where I am not giving anyone else the controls over my being. Every time I try to give a friend, an employer, some others as the reasons for my behavior, I am again giving up my controls and responsibility. I am denying my own choices. All the excuses I have to not be who I want to be, deny my affirming way. Finding the way, I have found, is different for everyone. There is no single path except the one that unfolds for each of us. There is no single magical place to get to. When I become my own controller, my garden assumes its own vital nature, freeing itself, freer and freer.

Affirming my child, my feelings, includes recognizing the ways I give others control over me. While opening to my feelings, sometimes small reactions others have to me, trigger gigantic responses. Other people's feelings and opinions have considerable impact. Revealing my child, I often feel as if I have no choices, surrounded by a circle of fear. It seems the buttons of my uncertain self are always being pushed. No matter which way I turn, others seem to be pulling my strings. Everyone seems to have control over me but me. As long as my heart is separated from my will, as long as the world stands between me and my child, it is no wonder I feel panicked, hopeless, overextended and fragile. Trying to separate my child, my feelings from the world about me, it is no wonder I am confused. Here is my child trying to jump up on my lap and my work, my friends, all my excuses to care for everything but me, stand in the way. My child is left standing amazed at how I give the world complete control over my feelings. It is as if I were a walking puppet with the world pushing my buttons, pulling my strings as it chooses. My child sits down and waits until I realize it is me who gives the world my buttons and strings to push and pull. He hopes instead of giving him to the world to take care of, I take care of him myself. Very quickly he reminds me how much fun it is for me to put him in the controls, pushing and pulling my own way.

The more I have my own controls, the less I need to control others. The more I accept my feelings and opinions as my own, I see others' feelings and opinions as theirs. I am changing my investment from others to myself. Wealth and other forms of security come most easily when I acknowledge the wealth and security I have inside. My child, my heart, and my head creating my way, the personal power I gain gives me security. Trusting my heart to unfold my way becomes my life's insurance.

As long as I accept my child only as much as the world accepts him, I am busy showing my new self to my friends and my family and I am setting them up once again to be my controllers. When I withdraw, isolating myself from others I'm also setting them up to control my path. The past and future are filled with controls over my being if I believe in them. Examining how I imagine others feel about me, I get in touch with how I give them power over my being.

Seeing how I use the past and future to limit myself in the present is another revealing exercise. I am always projecting my feelings, my child into the world. Then I try to recapture the parts of myself I have placed in the hands of others. I put my child on about everyone else's lap but my own. When my child feels uncertain, I turn to others and make them my controllers or I turn to myself. If I am happy and successful, everyone will assume credit for it. If I am lonely and sad, everyone is just as quick to say I'm responsible. When I push and pull my own strings and buttons, I receive the credit for

In a society where being unhappy is normal
Where struggle and compromise are expected, solicited
And rewarded, when I am relaxed and smiling
Others may view me as crazy.

But what is to be crazy or sane?
I know for myself
I feel crazy when I am not being
Who I want to be.

Imagine if
No one was allowed to be who they didn't want
To be?
What kind of world would we live in?

all my being. At times I am trying to prove to others how free I am. But I am just hoping they will accept me so I can more easily accept myself. Revealing myself is so complex when I place the world between me and my child.

My child is sick and tired of me using the world as my excuse for not caring for him. It seems whenever he really needs me, I am saying "Yes but, yes but I have to do this, yes but I am expected to be there, yes but I cannot change the plans . . ." I seem to be always projecting a circle of fear onto the world separating my child from me. This circle of fear may be clothed in lots of luxury and security but nevertheless exists limiting our reunion. My child cannot be denied wanting to be with me. Asking him what he wants, looking at my excuses for denying him, I discover my most current circle of fear.

Separating others from my child and myself, I become responsible for my feelings. However in the process my past relationships are being changed and I begin to appear to be different. In our society people who appear to be different in one form or another are communicated with as if they are crazy. Everybody has all these excuses to not be who they want to be. Social and psychological labels are very accessible for everyone who does not appear normally compromised and unhappy. Very soon I realize only I can determine what is normal and what is crazy for me. I know for myself, I feel crazy when I am being who I do not want to be. During the process of reuniting my will with my heart, only my feelings seem to be the best judge. When asked as a therapist what is crazy, I reply with my only rule: "no-one is allowed to be who they don't want to be." Except for prohibiting violence towards others, any behavior and feelings are okay if they are in pursuit of our will.

I have yet to meet someone who does not have some craziness. The most real people I know are those who are most open about the wonder and unknowing trust they have with their own lives. Sharing how unknowing we feel, we laugh with one another getting in touch with our circles of fear, each of our processes of trusting. All the excuses we have to limit ourselves begin standing in front of us, challenging us, making fun of our attempts to deny ourselves.

When I am ready, the world is no longer attacking or defending my experience. We are simply affirming one another. Instead of relating to what's wrong with the world and proceeding to struggle, I am relating to what's real. Loving the child in the world affirms my own feelings. Loving the sanity in others, I am validating my own. My life instead of being full of accidents and out of control seems to be filling with coincidences and a certain synchronicity. The pulse of my will seems to parallel the beat of my heart. My experience is an accumulation of trust creating personal power to create some more. I have heard of an Indian Medicine man who can control the weather by making rain. I enjoy believing in this possibility, becoming more and more in control of my world.

When the world stood between me and my child, I was always searching for happiness and magic. Now I am asking myself, why am I running so hard away from my garden? Why am I choosing to struggle? Why am I looking everywhere for my own magic? Why am I content with so little? By continuing the search, I am denying my heart and will being together. Denying my child, I am avoiding the sunshine, flowers, the garden ready for him to play. I amaze myself by the amount of energy and time I spend running from my heart in pursuit of someone else's or some substitute. I seem to have this craziness of being overly eager to jump into the circles of fear, holding onto my paralysis of will. I could be revealing myself, loving my child, melting my fear, holding him in my arms. Taking my child from the world's lap and putting him on my own, I see no reason to send him away again. My will is beating too strongly to do anything but follow my course.

Realizing my way
Sometimes I need to deny my way
Where I am all boxed in

Now someone can try to pull me out
But I cannot really be free until I'm ready

Accepting my need to deny my way
Trusting a seeming hopeless course
Can bring healing resolution.

Denying
the
Way

Realizing the way sometimes demands a course of denying my way, compromising, surrendering myself until I have had enough. No one's words or encouragement can help me change my way until I am ready. Accepting my need to deny myself, following a blind and destructive course can bring healing resolution. At times the only course I feel safe enough to be choosing is one of self denial. Whether I am hitting my head against the wall for good reason or not, acceptance by myself and by others of pursuing my own way, no matter where it's going, gives me the love and trust to find my own necessary course.

When I feel other's demands and needs controlling me, I often appease them and forgive them by following their way. I deny my way thinking it is the easiest course. I forgive others, proceeding on their route instead of forgiving myself, and begin returning to my path. Whenever my way is denied it is because of misplaced forgiveness. Instead of forgiving a way that is not me and continuing to follow it, why not forgive my weakened self and begin a path accordingly? Eventually, instead of placing my trust in a way which is not me, I will begin to trust again my own will, my own necessary course if I feel the love and trust to do so.

I deny myself whenever I begin believing in a course

which does not follow my heart. Every thought, every action towards another course reinforces its reality, denying the reality of my heart. Each word which is spoken from a place other than my heart gives support to a way other than my own. I may be wishing for love, fantasizing many happy adventures, waiting for some special event to happen, but I always live the life that I am living and prepared for. My day is a mirror of my expectations. If I think about being wealthy but live my life as if I am poor, prepared for more poverty, the real investment of myself is in being poor. I am denying my way. All of my excuses only make my self denial more easy. But it is my 'self' and I have the right to allow or deny it as I will.

My path is as full as I risk imagining and believing it can be. To begin with I am always denying my way by my lack of faith in trusting and believing in my own wishes. Upon loving my imagination, my heart feels embraced. With the love, I shortly find myself expecting my wishes. My world becomes as great as my vision. Unfolding my way begins with developing my vision. Self-denial ranges from suicide to not believing in our own imaginations. Who can say where self-denial begins and ends? Who can say what is permissible and what is not? Denying my way is a problem in my perception, a lack of vision.

Allowing or limiting myself, it's a question of believing in the basic order of things or believing life is basically an accident with occasional coincidences. With order as the assumption, everything amiss is realized as a temporary self-made illusion and teacher. With chaos ruling my beliefs, my life being disrupted becomes routine. Growing with, strengthening my belief in order everything out of harmony increasingly disappears as I realize the order in my disharmony and become free again. One assumption gives my will back to me. The other gives my heart to the whims of my life's events.

My words, thoughts, and actions come from my own intuitive center unless I do not feel safe enough to trust what I feel. When I am denying my way, I do not feel safe enough to listen to my real needs. Meanwhile my heart can provide every word, thought, and action if I trust its beat.

The weight of the world is as heavy as I need it to be until I realize it is weightless. The times denying my way are the times realizing the world's weight. The burdens I feel are my necessary teachers, challenging my will until I learn they no longer have control over me. If somebody takes these teachers from me I will need to find them someplace else. Ultimately it is the paths I take which deny my heart which hold the keys to me appreciating myself. The more lost I am, the greater the discovery upon again finding my way. Denying the way can hold all of life's beauty and mystery.

I have to do it all alone
But I do not have to be alone.

I can live changing and withdrawing
Feeling always separate from the world
Or I can live feeling and trusting
Creating a new world

Putting a home together within
I find a home coming together without.
The community within and without
Are reflections of me becoming my own.

The Community
Within
and
Without

I am always realizing my home, the garden within, the end to the mad journey outside of myself. As much as my relationship to my body and feelings illustrates the degree of fear or trust I have to follow my will, my relationships with others demonstrate whether my will is based upon fear and aggression or on faith and love. Much of this course appears as if it is just me, alone, looking for the real. The special relationships I was seeking in the world have been changed to a pursuit of a single way. The course of my heart has received all priority.

Initially the choice seemed to be just me, either changing the world or withdrawing from it. Either choice I felt controlled and overwhelmed me. Everywhere I turned, every relationship I entered, felt as if it was a repetition of my life of struggle, compromise, and surrender. My adult life sometimes consciously and often unconsciously was just a continuance of early traumas, of my first childhood. The decision to create another childhood includes the decision to create a new world, a new family to meet the needs of my unresolved feelings, to support my unfolding will.

An important part of realizing and resolving the early traumas that I am still projecting and acting out onto the world includes creating a new community to live in. It does not matter if this community is a nuclear family, extended family or a communal family. The important thing is that the family I have in my second childhood include the idea that the wishes and needs and responsibility to my child are as important as the needs of others. Secondly, loving my will back into my own is dependent upon providing my child with trusting relationships based upon honesty and need instead of power and control. Ending the mad journey outside of myself seems to be dependent upon trusting relationships providing me with the love to find my home again, within. Raising a child in the world demands if not a Mommy and Daddy at least a consistent trusting relationship with someone. Raising my child a second time demands no less. In the process of my second childhood I cannot be a child, friend, and guiding parent all at the same time. Creating a feeling of open and honest community around me allows for me to begin trusting my own way instead of remaining determined to change or withdraw from the old routines. A community around me helps me realize the lack of love I feel within, the lovelessness I am projecting onto the world.

As with other aspects of my second childhood, a community is not just arbitrarily put together but is part of my process of ending my old ways of relating. They were based more on the needs of others than my own and now I can begin to define and expect relationships which are more equally and honestly determined. The community itself, its size and shape does not determine my resolution. But the safe environment and the relationships that expect me to be who I am, provide the minimum for my child, heart, and head to become my own. The philosophy and structure of this community is less important than the trust and respect for my changing feelings and beliefs. Democratic means to solve problems arising within my second family supports me in working out my difficulties within. The more I exercise my will over my life, the safer my child feels to begin expressing his own. Within my community, I safely explore the fine line between my social responsibility to others and responsibility to myself. Instead of assuming I must always adjust, I begin learning that I create my environment. The task seems to be to have as much personal freedom as possible and few other obligations, all the while looking at and feeling the excuses I have to deny myself.

Upon deciding not to change or withdraw from the world based upon money, power relationships and credentials of many sorts, a new world is created. The commodity most respected becomes trust, everyone in pursuit of our own reality. Work is not for its own sake or for profit but for realizing my way. All the obstacles I encounter in the world are mirrors of the obstructions to my heart that I have within me. The closer my work is to the desires of my child, the closer my will is to being one with my heart. Instead of relating to my child through the world, I relate to him through the community around me.

Often it is difficult to know whether to respond to others or myself when the response would be different. A community helps me assume my controls including realizing my choices. I do not want to simply repeat the dramas of my first childhood within my second disguising it in a new family. The amount of trust and safety about me helps determine the love I can provide my child to discover his own way. Community means time for creative relationships, defining and expressing our needs and expectations to one another. This includes being together when together and being free to be a part when feeling apart. I have always been part of a community unknowingly, but my will has been too weak to realize it. My eyes have been too tired to find it. Conflicting messages of support and attack weakened my control over my day. A community around me supports the melting of the circles of fear which have been subverting my will. A community exposes the fear of me being alone against the world. In search of the community without, I feel my need for the community within. The two help realize one another. The community within meanwhile yearns for a community without to share and explore all my being. What child wants to grow up alone when other children are around to explore alleys and playgrounds together?

For either community, within or without, I know of no plan, no agenda for finding the way. Raising my child has a trusting process of opening unto my own. Yet at times my child needs structure, discipline, defined relationships or trust is not possible. Only a feeling community can know if my child needs love when he withdraws or needs to be held responsible for his actions. Finding the balance between responding to myself and others, devoting myself to my child and a community, opening my eyes to see the world without and being able to close my eyes to feel the world within is a fine and subtle path. I am open to feel love from others as I am able to love my child. Sometimes my child is able to accept my love in terms of what he feels only from others. In the community within and without, only through the expression of our mutual and differing wills do I experience my own necessary path.

Community, as organized or loose as it may be a group living together collectively or living together spread across the globe, living in a community helps me to realize my capacity of love. Receiving and giving, revealing and denying, seeking and withdrawing, my community loves me to trust myself. The world within and without continually mirror one another. I am always looking towards a more exact image, only to know I am becoming my changing self. The trust I have in my will, I find in the hearts of others. The faith or judgment I have for others is always a statement about myself. I am unleashing my will living in the community within and without, being, reflecting, becoming whole.

Sometimes when I take it all
And put it down
I am doing the nicest thing
For me.

The River of my Life

Some people spend their lives thinking
Thinking until they understand.
Other people are convinced feeling and feeling until it is felt
Will set them free.
All I know after thinking
Is something about thinking.
After feeling
I know something about feeling.
For me it is the thinking itself,
My doing, my feeling which is important.
It is where I stand now
Placing my feet on the river's bottom
That ultimately counts.

The moment I want is now
Because this is where I always am.
I am really never anyplace else.

The
Heart
of
Play

There are so many ways to be. And there are so many ways to be caught in the river of life. Sometimes I have endless thoughts, each one convinced more than the thought preceding, how justified it is. Meanwhile I remain stuck somewhere in life's mud. If I am not thinking, I am often doing, doing, and doing quite determined to get someplace other than where I am. But instead of flowing down life's river as I wish, I am doing, pushing and pulling, disrupting my current further. Every time I am thinking and thinking, or doing and doing, quite involved and dedicated to my efforts, I remain open to forgetting who I really am right now. It becomes difficult to remember that when I am overwhelmed or stuck, my problem may be as simple as realizing I am thinking and thinking or doing and doing instead of being as I want to be right now. When my busy mind or my busy self is not being as I want, I quickly find many excuses trying to believe in themselves so I can continue being who I do not want to be. I am perpetually yearning, edging, grasping, withdrawing, dancing an infinite number of dances. As easily as the days pass, my words pass and life's costumes along with them. But I am still either caught or free in the river of my life.

Some people spend their lives thinking until they understand. But after I am done thinking all I can really say I know something about it is thinking. Other people are convinced feeling and feeling until something is felt will set them free. But when I am feeling I do not know whether I am denying or allowing who I am right now in the present. All I am certain of is that I am feeling. For me it is the thinking itself, my doing, my feeling which is important. It is where I stand now, placing my feet on the river's bottom that ultimately counts. The moment now I want because this is where I always am. I am really never anyplace else. Each thought, each act, each feeling is the stand I'm taking in the midst of my heart's flow. My feelings, thoughts, and acts can be the shoreline of my heart's stream. Or they can be obstacles, the dams blocking my will's fulfillment. My thoughts, acts, and feelings revealing nothing more than themselves, it is my experience of the stands I take which support or limit my way.

Thinking and thinking or doing and doing
I may be stuck in life's mud
Forgetting about being
Who I want to be.

If I can care for my life's moments, smile at them, pick them up and laugh at them, if I can play with my way, then I know I'm with my heart's stream, swimming, diving, floating, stroking my stroke.

Play keeps my thoughts in touch with my feelings and will, my head in touch with my child and heart. Play laughs at myself when my thoughts are too serious and when I am believing I am forever overwhelmed with emotion. Play is always a ready door, more often no door at all, keeping me open for more play, more experience. Play never threatens itself, never limits my way. Play enjoys more play as my heart enjoys fulfilling itself. Pumping through all of me, play puts my head, heart, and child in the same house, under the same roof.

When my mind is seized in thought or my child is overtaken with feeling, play reminds me my heart is my life's source. The world is without enemies with play. With play, I am never helpless. I cannot continue doing and doing endlessly. I cannot think and think without resolution with play. Any time, any path which includes play cannot fall into the bottomless pit of taking itself too seriously. Play can only laugh at itself and move on. Play's course unleashes wisdom and feeling, the wisdom and feeling we brought into the world. Play exposes the madness of the world without entering into it. Play always building trust and faith has no need to control others, especially those who choose not to play.

Self importance, self indulgence all of my excuses to deny the real—play seduces. Play is the enemy of self pity. And self pity is the basic game of all play. When I can look at my life's reflection and laugh, I know I have won. Play always introduces the next move.

The human kingdom of boredom, like that of believing in self importance, is eaten by play. Wishing and fantasizing are play's toys, always creating more. When I am playing I am asking for what I want and believing I deserve to have it. When I am playing I have it too. I have it all.

Play teases and loves my heart to reveal more and more. My will's natural stream takes over, flooding all the reticent parts of my life. The endless dialogues with myself, with the past, the dream which has grown empty, are erased with play. Play is what facilitates letting go and creating anew. Dogma, doubt, dispute can hardly continue. Business, lunch and conversation are exposed for what they are. Everything is exposed, even the exposing. Play surfaces the real, the hidden depths, the nakedness in the obvious. Play always on the attack against self limiting ways of thinking and feeling, yields more and more space to be.

The heart of play is overflowing. Within the serious world of painful struggle is always the heart of play somewhere playing.

Play is the enemy of self pity
And self pity is the basic game of all play.
When I am looking at my life's reflection
And laugh, I know I have won.

Play always introduces the next move.

Living
the
Fantasy

I feel her, resting on my shoulder during the day. I am always fantasizing and lying awake. She is the size of a leaf and as powerful as an entire forest. Sometimes she comes to me in a woman's body, greets me and hugs me hello. Other times I'm walking through a meadow, she sneaks up on me, hiding in the wind. We love each other. She dances in my dreams when I am sad. If I breathe deeply and close my eyes I hear her whispering. I am reminded that in order to be in order I must believe. When I open myself to the magic I see her dark silver hair and find her circling around me in restaurants and a dirty parking lot. I smile feeling her knowing, I know. She's here. She's here. Its like sleeping between the sky and the sea, sleeping with the sun. Running ever so slowly, flying between the footsteps from my soul to my mind, like the loud sounds of a quiet pond, the moments stuck between moments, we are always playing. We are exploding as softly as I choose. She is my lover. I allow her and feel her inside of me and outside of me. She is when I want her. She is the second conversation in every conversation. I know her laughing, laughing through the world.

She follows me to the bank. I am waiting in line when she is licking inside of my ear. "I love you. I love you." I look around to see if anyone else has heard her. She peeks at me from behind the teller's hair. The teller smiles, "You look like life is going your way?" I smile in return. "Just being nice to myself," as I disappear.

I am constantly choosing this moment, right now. What do I want? I see her in the eyes of a black bird in front of me. I am inside of the black bird looking back at me. I'm flying through and away . . . landing back in my body. Where does it all begin and end? She sits patiently, as I doubt, as I try to scare myself. I feel her tugging at my hand when I'm getting bogged down with myself or friends. We are always following one another. I continue loving myself. I take off and land in her lap. The love I have will not settle down. When I search for limits and reasons for the flight, I feel her softly teaching. She gives me the controls, the secret powers whenever I reach for them. I am ready. She is in front of me, also ready. My body is the bridge. It's the spirit, my spirit and the world. She is standing on top of my senses always ready to give me more. Every time she is here. I feel her, resting on my shoulder during the day . . .

I am always fantasizing. When I am centered upon my path, my will is unfolding my greatest fantasy. Consciously or not my life is a fantasy. All I can really know of the world is what I imagine. Others are certain the world is this way or that. But all I am certain about is my world, my experience. The question becomes whether I am going to believe and follow my fantasy of the world or someone else's? As a child I was always fantasizing. Indeed where one world ended and another began was never quite clear. I was in one world until others determined it necessary for me to be otherwise. But no matter how similar or dissimilar my path becomes to everyone around me, it is still only a path, only how I imagine the world to be, only how I experience the real, saying nothing of how much of reality I am not experiencing or covering up.

Thus if I am going to follow a path, live out a fantasy, I see no reason for not living out the most outrageous fantasy I can imagine. Believing in my fantasies is the surest way of believing in my child. Pursuing my fantasies is the most direct route to my heart. What's between me and my fantasies is my circle of fear created by the frustration of my will.

The parts of my life that I have seemingly no control over are the things which I have given up fantasizing about. In order to gain control, I begin by fantasizing how I would like these parts of my life. Fantasy reminds me that I create my reality and reality is as I expect it.

When someone approaches me for help
Instead of telling him his problem
And giving him my solutions
I listen and ask him to fantasize his desired resolution.

Once he knows what he wants
And believes he deserves it
The weight of his problem
Is shifted to the fantasy.

Loving each other to find our own necessary way
A healing process which is our own takes place. . .

Everything in my life I cannot give up, every relationship that I cannot imagine myself separate from or without, are other parts of my life that I am denying my unfolding fantasy, giving others my controls instead. I am stuck, holding onto, feeling my paralysis of will instead of trusting my unfolding fantasy to be and become. Every relationship I can imagine myself separate from allows me to appreciate that relationship so much more. Otherwise my hunger has just become overwhelming and the relationship a habit, an addiction, a fix instead of a growing, freeing experience. Believing in my fantasies is the first step in the process of gaining control over my life, keeping my relationships, my life in tune with my desires.

When someone approaches me for therapy or for help, instead of hearing their problem and giving them my solutions, the techniques and answers I have found for myself, I have them fantasize their choices, their most desired course, how they would like their life to be. Getting from their problem, their current paralysis of will, to their fantasy, their will beating the strongest, is what life becomes about.

My fantasy and my path is not important. What matters now is that each of us have a fantasy and create a path accordingly. So many people have been following everyone else's course, believing in the world as everyone around them, that they no longer have a fantasy, much less believe they deserve it. For them it is a process of relearning what they want, rediscovering their child, their feelings. Fortunately most people know what they don't want. So it is only time until they can imagine how they really want to feel and live.

When negative or frightening fantasies arise in my mind, it is just parts of my unresolved will experiencing itself. Better to experience these parts in fantasy versus needing to materialize these negative experiences in order to reach some resolution. Trusting my heart to melt the obstructions in my way, is the most simple and direct course.

Once I have had a fantasy, there is a part of me which will rush out in the world, struggling to prove once again there is hope for my child. I become determined to show my heart is not under attack. But, too often my charges into the world only repeat the traumas and disappointments of my original childhood, setting it all up once again. Exploring my excuses for not accepting my fantasies and loving my fantasies as they are, as just fantasies, is the important beginning for merging the world with my wishes. If I can enjoy my desires, just as desires, before they are actualized or not, realizing my fantasy as being important in and of itself, my child and heart move closer. Life is getting to a place believing I deserve my fantasies. Once I believe I deserve my fantasies the world no longer has control over my being. My circles of fear are melted. Once I realize the world is not controlling my fantasy, my fantasy comes true. From a point of view that life is a struggle, this magic seems impossible and a lie. Indeed from that point of view, living one's fantasy is very far removed. But when my heart and will are beating together, living my fantasy is the most natural thing for me to do.

In the past I would think about what I wanted and proceed to struggle in the world to attain it. The world stood between me and my child. Life was always just out of reach. Now, loving my child, the source of my fantasy, believing in the marriage of my child's wishes and my will's strength, my heart unfolds the path of easiest effort and greatest living. Once I believe in my fantasies, I just expect them to unfold. The mystery is not out in the world but within the world, my heart. My greatest wishes are mine once I release the world's grasp upon my will.

Recently in a small town in northern California, I was brewing magic with a special ally and friend. We were discussing how we wanted to spend the winter. Together we announced, "Why not live abroad, work and later travel?" He suggested we advertise in the Wall Street Journal as sorcerers seeking employment with an international corporation. I reminded him we have to be careful what we fantasize because once we believe in it and accept it, it will come true. An international corporation sounded too formal and unfeeling for our kind of pursuit. "Why not work with a clinic or community abroad as therapists and then travel," I suggested. We smiled and meditated together, fantasizing our wishes to their fullest, trusting everything to unfold. Forty-eight hours later we were having dinner in this same small town when we heard that there was a German doctor in town looking for two therapists to come work with him in Europe. I looked at my friend and we smiled. The German doctor as it turned out, was looking for people to stay for four years, and who had different degrees and backgrounds than ours. But his fantasy was not going to interrupt my own. I told him I would be willing to come with a couple of important allies for many months. Having already accepted and expected my fantasy it was not a matter of negotiation but being open for this opportunity or the next to bring my fantasy to reality. As everything happened this meeting resulted in realization of our desires.

Looking out into the world
I see the fantasy
I am giving meaning to
Every day.

Looking out into the world
I see the world I feel inside
In the faces and voices I live with
Every day.

Looking out into the world
I see the garden,
When I realize the garden within,
Is ready to be out in the world.

If life is only a fantasy I see no reason why I should not take charge of my fantasy and create the one that really expresses my will, moment by moment. I become a warrior of sorts in pursuit of my heart. I do not go looking for obstructions or enemies. I do not go looking for fear. I accumulate my energies and love in search of my heart. When anything arises in my path I realize I have on some level of my being chosen this obstruction to experience and challenge my failing will. My enemies? The world has not determined my course but my child, seeking his resolution, and my heart coming together. As a warrior my heart and child always remain in sight of one another. The world does not interfere with my vision. The world is just the forest, the arena of my unfolding self determination. My excuses to deny my quest, my fantasies, always tell me the boundaries I am setting to my reality. My fears express my desires for pain. It is all right to desire pain. It may be an important part of my resolution. It is all a necessary fantasy. Eventually instead of choosing the accepted fantasies of pain and struggle, I will create another way. Loving my fantasies I begin leaving fantasies of pain choosing ways of love instead.

The warrior loves the hold that fear has over his heart. Fantasies are naturally released. My fear is my belief in attack. I am always taking back the controls I give the world over my being. Loving my fantasies I soon know I am creating my way, no longer believing in attack.

When I cannot fantasize I am overwhelmed with fear. My child does not feel safe enough to even imagine what he would like. Getting my child to a place that he is always fantasizing, believing he deserves his wishes, I'm freeing, letting go of my will. I begin by giving him permission to not know, to know only what he does not want, to be angry, feel hurt, and confused. My heart will always lead me to my resolution when I am ready to allow it.

Loving my fantasy, I begin loving the world. The world is only my heart undressed. Everything in the world I withdraw from or dislike are parts of my fantasy, my heart, that I am unwilling to accept or take charge over and change. Realizing my fantasy, I am realizing my heart instead of pretending to realize someone else's. The world I see is but my most accepted fantasy of the moment. As a warrior, knowing, accepting, nurturing the source of my path, my creative center, living my fantasy, I am lifting the veil surrounding my heart. As I unfold my heart creating my world I begin seeing it as it really is without interpretations. As looking in-

Awakening to the Dream

I am always dreaming. My dream is the road of my will and my feelings coming together. Awake or asleep, I am dreaming. My dream beckons me to enter. The closer I am to my dream, the closer I am to my life as it is happening. During the day when I awaken I am still dreaming for everything I am experiencing is a part of my unfolding psyche. At night I continue nurturing my child and heart by dreaming.

Once my child and heart dreamed day and night. But gradually my feelings and will were crowded more and more into seeking their resolution in my sleep as I dreamed. Rediscovering my child and heart, I'm relearning I feel all the time. The road of my feelings is my dream. Dreaming expresses the world of my child and heart. I am learning how to dream once again, their dream.

At one time there was no difference between dreaming, feeling, fantasies, being awake or asleep. The world and I, all were part of the same, my experience. Gradually I learned to separate myself from parts of my world which did not meet other's expectations. Dreams were told to be something that occurred at night and somehow not very important or real. My dream's events as the events of my life in general were of primary concern. My feelings, my experience of my dream was secondary. The ability to dream and capture my heart

I am always dreaming.
My dream is the road of my will and my feelings
Coming together.
Awake or asleep, I am dreaming.
My dream beckons me to enter.

The closer I am to my dream,
The closer I am to my life
As it is happening.

Day and night
Dreaming
I am experiencing
My unfolding psyche.

My child and my heart
Are nurtured
By dreaming.
I am always dreaming.

wrestling and joining my child was left to me to someday pursue, as I pursue my feelings and will in general.

My life's plot, my daily behavior is no longer paramount when I begin recognizing my experience, my dream, the internal drama containing the doorways to my path. Dreaming is the most direct approach to reality. My dream and experiences are real for me as other's dreams are real for them. The fathers of Psychology say "dreams lead to the soul itself." My dream teaches the way to my heart. Trusting its unwinding and sometimes difficult course, is trusting the opening of my will.

Whether dreaming awake or asleep, it is the moments which feel out of control, the moments I feel I have no choice which deserve my greatest attention and care. The actual events or plot of my dream is less important. My experience of the events speaks of my separations, the separations from myself. My dream is the world which is my will unfolding. And it is loving, nurturing, my seemingly helpless times that I find and develop my dream and the source of my inner strength and freedom. Dreaming, loving my dream unfolding is the acceptance and caring for my most basic self rising from the depths of my being.

If the world was not a part of my own psyche how could I be experiencing it? Since I am experiencing the world, why not own my experience as mine, open to it, permit it, take care of it, be with it as parts of myself? The separations I feel from others awake or asleep are my own separations. My dream is the healing process between my child and my heart. Dreaming, my feelings and will become one.

As I witness the symbols of my dream coming together and battling with each other during the day and the night, I witness the people and events of my experience acting out the roles of my will and feelings resolving. The varying parts of myself are always emerging and disappearing, rising and sinking into the mystery of my psyche. My dream is the integration.

Dreaming, sometimes I am so desperately trying to disown, separate myself from my life. I try to escape from the experiences my dream seems to be demanding that I become aware of. I can change the events in my dream day after day. I can run from my dream as I run from parts of myself in general. But the darker sides of my heart, my fear always rings through sooner or later. The closer I am to my dream, the closer I am to reality, feeling and resolving my child and will. Realizing my dream's experience, the differing forces, assuming all of my dream's feelings as parts of me introducing themselves, seeking my attention, the more complete, in control and one with myself I am. The real dream becomes the dream in which I have the courage to live my life fully as a dream. Everything within my experience is as parts of my greater self, taking the reins, creating the most beautiful dream possible.

Several weeks ago I was dreaming of a special girlfriend in America. We were sharing our lives, feeling very relaxed with one another. I realized I was dreaming, being in Germany and she was in America. But everything seemed so real, so lucid and immediate. Can I enjoy this even if it is a dream? We take a long walk in the woods holding each other's hand. She picks up a stone and gives it to me. I feel its smooth edges between my fingers. We return home and I grow sad thinking this is all only a dream. I'm afraid it's all a lie and my firend really isn't with me. I go lay in the corner. My friend asks what's wrong? I explain to her this is all not real because I am dreaming. I want her to hold me. But everything feels futile. She picks me up and holds me anyway. Suddenly again everything feels as real as real can be. Next I am aware I'm sitting in bed. On the floor I see the necklace she had given me somehow having gotten out of a special bag on my desk many feet away. One bead is broken as I am grasping, scrambling to know the real. How can I believe my friend wasn't here? Where does reality and dreaming begin and end?

Dreaming shows me the world as it really is, before looking through the lens of general viewing. Merging with my dream I am merging with my creative and pumping source. My child and my heart together, dreaming generates my power to create my own reality. I become the base of interpretation.

Before rediscovering my child, my dream awake or asleep was out of control, chaotic, unintelligible. When I tried to impose some order on my dream during the day, my child scrambled at night determined to show his unsettledness. A great part of me was afraid of my dream awake and asleep as I was afraid of my feelings in general. I found all sorts of excuses to avoid responsibility, responding to my dream. Loving my child, relearning to trust my feelings, my dream takes on new importance. My dream expresses my child's and my heart's true state. Suddenly the people in my dream appear as I really know them. The different realities between my head and child are becoming one.

Now when I am out of touch with my dream, I know I am seeing everyone and everything as it pretends to be and not as I really experience and know it. Relearning to dream I am seeing the world as it really is. Dreaming, I am experiencing and taking back my controls, seeing my own reality. I am dreaming my dream, living my path instead of joining other's dream they are acting out in the world. I am awakening to the dream, being with the world as I really am.

The Real Dream

The real dream
Becomes the dream in which I have
The courage to live my life fully
As a dream.

As with feelings, my dream is for me to initially recognize, accept and nurture. Ultimately as with feelings, my dream is for me to change, take charge over and dream my most satisfying dream moment by moment. Loving my dream, my feelings, my emerging child and heart brings me to trusting the world as it is. I no longer have to pretend to be part of the mass dream encompassing the world when it is not who I am. I am no longer separated from the truth by many circles of fear. When I am scared that is my opportunity to hold and move closer to the source of my dream. Dreaming, the world's grasp is losing its hold over me. I am coming into my own dream.

Dreaming unlocks my greater will. As I approach my heart closer and closer literally I merge with the beating spring of my center. I begin dreaming brighter colors, golden yellow and white. The further from my heart, the darker and duller are the colors of my experience. Beginning to recognize and follow the brighter way, my experience, is following my heart.

Capturing my dream allows me to love the fullest way. Being in the world as it really appears to me allows me to relate to it and love as I really feel. Children feel and love naturally until they are told some feelings, some love is not all right. Now I am supporting my child to feel and love, dreaming his own dream. Since the world and I are joined together in my dream, it is not a question of taking and giving love but sharing the love I am finding in my heart and the world. Dreaming, my heart and the world realize our common bond.

Before rediscovering my child, my dream seemed out of reach and often unimportant as the way I often related to my feelings. I had given up on my child including my dream for other ways. As relearning to feel, relearning to dream becomes less and less overwhelming and more an expected path of living.

To begin with I become aware of and control my dream at night by becoming aware of and determining my dream during the day. How can I expect to be with my dream at night if during the day I am far from my feelings and determining my course? Loving the path closest to my heart centers me more in my dream day and night. Disturbing events at any time during my dream are warning signals for me to become closer to my heart. I am feeling now. I am dreaming now. I can give my environment the controls to change and interpret my dream. Or I can find my own with others supporting me to find my way. If I don't like my dream, I learn how to change it. During the day if I don't like what's occurring in a relationship I reapproach it and change it. At night when I don't like what I am experiencing again I can reapproach it and redream it. I settle back into the experience remembering how it was while imagining how I want everything to be. Consciously I re-enter the dream and change it, dreaming it the way I want until I am satisfied. Gradually with my dream day or night I will be able to correct its course as soon as it is not as I desire. As I become more and more responsible, I respond quicker to my dream.

The other night I awakened in my sleep in fright. Just moments before I had been hanging on a cliff, alone and afraid. Upon awaking I shivered with my fear and then decided I was not going to accept this dream. I sunk back into a state half awake, half asleep and started redoing my dream. I imagined myself hanging as the dream slowly began re-emerging. But now the forest service was there throwing me a rope, easing my fall to the ground.

The same day I had a painful conversation with the director of the clinic. Hours later with the tension still gripping me, I decided to change my dream. I sunk back into imagining the conversation but this time it went as I wanted and deserved it to be. I felt my feelings taking back their power from the controlling figure in the dream. I felt how I separated myself from the director, centering on our differences thus separating me from my dream, from myself. Feeling him as a part of me, pushing and pulling my course, I gain control, understanding of what really happened. The world is not separate from me or I suffer being separated from myself. Redreaming my dream day or night I am affirming the will of my heart and child coming together.

Pain challenges the way of dreaming as it tries to make

itself real and the dream somehow not. The attacks upon myself are the ultimate obstacles to my will. Pain leads the attack, trying to keep me out of control impressing upon me that I am surrendered by something other than myself. To begin with I start to redream about the pain, dreaming it is located in another place. Just by moving its location I begin taking my power back from its convincing message. So instead of my neck hurting, I begin dreaming I have hurt my shoulder. Soon the pain has moved and in the process I have begun to assume control over it. The pain may be no less but I have controlled its location. I can keep moving the pain from one area to another until I am ready to begin dreaming there is no pain at all. Through dreaming I begin realizing that the world including my body is the stage where I am presenting myself, along with the limits and strengths I am attaching to my being.

If I don't like my dream
I learn to change it.

During the day if I don't like what's occurring
In a relationship I reapproach it and change it.
At night when I don't like what I'm experiencing
Again I reapproach it and redream it.

Consciously I re-enter the dream
Day or night and change it,
Dreaming it the way
I want until I feel satisfied.

Remembering that the store line I am waiting in, the road I am driving, the meal I am eating, that every experience is part of my psyche, my dream, helps me draw closer to my life and understand that I am creating my own reality. I may not control all the events I am a part of but I am determining my experience. I am experiencing my dream. There is no reason not to feel it, change it if I want, and live it, breathing it to my fullest.

Relearning to dream is relearning to see the world as symbols of my unfolding psyche. As others interpret their dream, I am always learning to interpret and shape my dream for me as I am learning to care for my feelings. My dream as my child is for me to relearn to respond to. Responding to my day and night activity, I am uniting my heart and the world.

I am always dreaming, redreaming, dreaming and redreaming until I am the center of my will. My dream is a training ground, a source of fantasy and information for guidance. Dreaming is piercing the window to my most uncensored desires and anxieties, landing in the treasury of my soul's wealth. As I build my life from a place of having my desires and caring for my anxieties, my dream becomes the pool from which to create. Dreaming is my most basic self emerging for me to resolve the old and begin choosing the new. The closer I am with my dream until I am actually with it and in it as I choose, running my course, the closer life approaches its true reality of dreaming. My waking state and sleeping experience merge. Leaping into the source of my limits, I am becoming conscious of myself, awakening to the dream.

If I want to see the world
I close my eyes.
If I want to hear the world
I plug my ears.
If I want to taste and smell the world
I close my mouth and nose.
If I want to touch the world
I sit still.

Everything *else just spoils me*
And helps me
To find
Myself!

Shamanic Initiation

If realizing the Shamanic is anything more than realizing the real, how could it be true? Yet all sorts of unnatural means are attempted in order to get a glimpse of its mystery. The more strange the phenomenon being sought, the more strange and greater lengths are believed necessary to be taken to get there. Yet it is only logical, the greater the act of power, the more simple the action required. Reducing reality, simplifying life, opens life for risking and creating as it is beating. The Shamanic awaits in one's responsibility to the moment.

Too often, all the veils, all the escapes into thinking and doing cover and recover, hide upon what is already hidden. A heart and a child, the home and source of life is overlooked. People whose lives are spinning out of control refuse to accept such a simple concept as a child and a heart waiting inside for their recognition. But stopping and making contact with the source of feeling and will confronts all self limiting ways of thinking, behaving, denying the world. Instead of being an adult who is out of control becoming a child and experiencing my inability to be responsible, allows me to become an adult again, responding to the world. The world beyond is realized by being in the world I'm in. The Shamanic begins when I stop kicking and running, shouting and hiding from what is here.

Initiation into the Shamanic involves living the death and rebirth experiences of everyday life. Everytime I let go of something controlling my heart and begin again, a death and rebirth occurs. More important than searching for and following some person of knowledge is my ability to know the end and beginning of my experiences. The Shaman awaits inside of everyone willing to let go of pain and to risk the joy. Its magic is no further than the out of control moments in each day being allowed to die and be reborn into new experience.

Within the process of relearning how to feel and direct one's will a birth experience takes place. In psychology, new therapies are guiding people back into literally re-experiencing birth with unspoken or indefinite promises of rebirth occurring with the event. For me the process of rediscovering my childhood and letting go of deep pains buried within, was dependent, from the beginning, upon my creation of new ways, revitalizing my will. The length of the process and necessity of re-experiencing birth or any single trauma of being out of control, was not as important as developing my will to feel my pain, letting something die within me in order to feel reborn creating once again. My resolution lies not within my pain, the death of all the unnecessary weight I carry, but in my ability to let go and create, to die and be reborn. My resolution when looked another way is to give birth and rebirth. Accepting my experiences both of pain and joy is being born and reborn to new experience.

On the road of developing my heart and child, becoming in control, I found myself re-experiencing my life when I was most out of control, when I was most a victim of events. Before I was capable of consciously being responsible for how I felt, I found myself feeling the terror and pain of being thrust out in the world as an independent, functioning being.

I use the words "found myself" because the experience started as if I was not in control, just trusting a process I had started months before. I decided to trust the experience mostly because I felt I had no choice. After about six months of rediscovering my child, I started feeling physical pains all over my body. The more love and support I felt in the pre-

The Shamanic
Awaits in my responsibility
To the moment.

The world beyond
Is realized
By being
In the world I'm in.

The Shamanic
Begins when I stop kicking and running
Shouting and hiding
From what is here.

sent from a girlfriend and other friends, the more intense these physical pains became. During the day all my ordinary activities were feeling split, conscious of themselves. I was feeling as if half of every experience was routine and the other half out of control. I was having nightmares of dreaming I was dreaming and waking, not knowing if I was still asleep or not. I would start screaming in my sleep thinking I was awake, waking meanwhile terrified, out of control. It was only the support of my friends that gave me support to stay with this process that continued.

When I would lie down and breathe into the physical pains, I rolled up into a tiny ball, feeling squeezed, pushed and pulled. Walls of pain seemed to come off the sides of my body. Small, little cries would come out of my mouth. My entire body would be sweating. The feelings associated with the pain were feeling totally unwanted, ugly, separated from the world. During the day I was overwhelmed in a state of feeling inbetween, stuck, being neither determined or undetermined. A blah feeling I had felt most of my life, feeling dulled intensified. This and a basic message I grew older with of feeling undeserving and separated from others became conscious and integrated as this birth experience unfolded. A part of me which felt forever out of touch became realized and slowly resolved.

As this experience continued off and on for weeks, I felt as if I was against a wall, surrendered, permanently compromised. Lights and noises took on great magnitudes of disturbance. Rejections from my girlfriend and other undesired events during the day would trigger this early trauma. All of my being felt over sensitive. Sometimes I would just lie on the floor and make grunts like animal noises, my body seemingly boiling and writhing, feeling partly conscious and partly stuck someplace else as if in some primeval state. Once I spent thirty hours in a small room unable to move. The pain was just climbing off every cell in my body and it felt so releasing to let it go. Just moments of my birth could be felt at one time.

Gradually I became aware the nightmare of struggle, of feeling out of control, was ending as I began responding to the pain, became responsible. My heart began beating stronger urging me to risk being more and reaching for what I wanted. Sharp pains occurred in my back as I tested my desires in the world. My face felt squeezed as I began to ask more from others. My arms and legs at different times felt twisted as I went in and out of feeling I can choose my experience. I began standing up for my needs. I started being nicer to myself, eating, sleeping, doing more what I wanted. One day I rolled up on a water bed and started feeling very little, just rocking softly, gently on the warm waves. I was feeling safe. Often I started gasping for air, feeling I couldn't breathe. Later I was to find out that when I was born my mother had pneumonia. Indeed we both did have a lack of air. Re-experiencing the terror, my need for air, my feelings of utter helplessness began to disappear. Something in my heart, my will would urge me to take care of myself from a very simple place, perhaps just a warm bath. Candles often centered my attention.

From this very simple place I began to understand how my life had been compromised because my will had been compromised in the beginning. I realized why I chose relationships which did not meet my needs, having my failing will re-experiencing itself. My life appeared as a rational and subjective extension of my earliest trauma of being out of control. Ordinary events were full of lots of symbolic meaning. As the grasp upon my heart was let go, I felt the events of the day no longer controlling how I feel. That was my biggest discovery. With this security I was feeling renewed, somehow attached and invested in myself and detached and uninvested from others. My relationship with my family felt different. I began choosing the kind of relationship I wanted instead of assuming it was the other way around. On some levels of my being I began to feel and understand how I chose my relationship with my parents from the beginning. I began to understand how I chose my experience to the events of my life. My parents were no longer responsible. I wanted to or gave up my determination from the beginning. It is as if the spirit within me needed my life's events in order to experience itself, fulfill some basic need for resolution. From some part of myself, I feel I chose not only my relationship with my parents, but having actually my parents as parents. Reliving my birth was a process of letting go of my experience that I am controlled by the world to being reborn determining my way.

Suddenly, however, the weeks of feeling moments of absolutely being curled up in pain waiting and eventually coming through some canal to life were no more important than momentary flashes of understanding that I am chosing my experience right now and if I do not like it, I am free to chose another. The re-experiencing of birth only allowed me to more fully understand the dieing and rebirth process I am always in. No experience was realized for being more important than another. Only my ability to experience, let go and create again seems to matter. The process does not end but begin and end, begin and end, begin and begin and begin. The re-experiencing of birth in itself led me nowhere but feeling helpless and out of control. But trusting, following my heart even through this time of seemingly endless craziness and pain in the way I needed to experience it, revitalized my will greatly. Others supporting me instead of trying to change my will was central.

At one time I found myself
Re-experiencing being thrust out into the world.
Small little cries would come out of my mouth.
My entire body would be writhing.

Finally my heart began beating stronger
Urging me to risk being more,
To reach out for what I want
To take care of myself from a very simple place.

I began to understand how my life had been compromised
Because my will had been compromised
As the grasp upon my heart was let go
I felt the events of my day controlling less how I feel.

Re-experiencing birth in itself may not be important
But my ability to experience
To let go and create again
Seems to matter.

A year later I was in California on a ranch attending the opening planning seminar for graduate school. In my class was Doris, a psychic healer, a Shaman from Alaska. One day I wandered to a cabin on the other side of the ranch. I laid down and began to cry, feeling lonely as a very little boy. As I cried I felt Doris' presence in the room. I just believed I was mistaking this feeling for my need of a mother right then. Doris' presence meanwhile comes and sits next to me, comforts me. I feel better, returning almost unnoticed back to the seminar. Doris looks up at me. As I look into her eyes, I know she knows where and how I have been. She walks over to me asking if I am all right, proceeding to tell me everything that she observed a few minutes before in the cabin. She says, "I would have come physically but didn't want to disturb you."

Instantly the moments of feeling Doris' presence in the room, her questioning me about my feelings afterwards, killed and gave birth to as much of my being as weeks and weeks of refeeling my birth a year before. Within minutes, everything I held true was scrambling for something to hold onto. I wanted to deny the whole experience but too much of me could not allow it. The best choice was to die and then feel life's new possibilities.

During the following week, event after unexplainable event took place in Doris' vicinity. Another member of my class, an executive from a major corporation found himself catching Eskimo words out of the air and giving them to Doris to finish a message she was receiving from her Shaman in the wilderness of Alaska. Doris smiled and laughed meanwhile with my uncertainty and awkwardness. I felt like I recognized this energy like recognizing feelings long ago forgotten. A part of me wanted Doris to immediately become my parent and teach me. I'm very skeptical about anything I cannot see and touch, so scared and excited. All of my beliefs about the world were shaking. Despite my feelings, somewhere I have always known there was more, hasn't everyone? Doris denied my attempts to have her assume control over my life. She laughed and welcomed my attempts to find my own way.

With that understanding I became her apprentice and she became my catalyst to more reality. Sometimes she would enter my dream while asleep and greet me and talk to me. When my beliefs would allow her, she would enter my dream while awake and send her gentle feeling all around me, sometimes leaving words in my mouth. Once she spent eight days with me in Colorado. Each day I wanted her to tell me, share something more, show me, what next should I do? But all she did was smile and make small talk, forcing me into trusting my own way. There has never been a better lesson.

During this time, since my initiation to a Shaman, I have begun to know death as knowing a best friend. Every hold on my being, the beliefs and feelings I let go of, has introduced me into new reality. Recognizing death's ways sometimes each day, sometimes moment by moment sets me free, fleeing into the Shamanic where there are no limits but those which I am yet afraid to let die. It has not been a question of having no limits, no attachments, no needs but following my heart, being able to let go of struggling and therefore able to enjoy them fully. The Shamanic demands I give up nothing. The only thing I must let go of is my belief that to live fully I must give up part of my being. The Shamanic is always challenging my friendship with death. Together we know this friendship is whipped into being by my fear. My fear of death is always being played in my fear of letting go of the circles of limits surrounding me. Death becomes my friend, because he introduces me to my encircled will. Death parts whenever I am holding onto the real. The Shamanic is life most grounded. Death blooms with confusion, probing, poking, posing all around me, keeping me determined in my will choosing precisely. Recognizing it, strengthens my heart more than almost any relationship. Sometimes when death and I see each other, shouting and screaming our desires—we stand free of one another, perhaps just for a holy instant, loving one another, being who we are.

Death stands around me in every unwanted experience. It tries to overwhelm me while I look for escape. Every road of struggle, surrender, compromise which is bidding for my will is death's seductive dance. Death thrives upon my fears, holding me in its arms when I do not see, feel, and touch my being. Its dark cloud encompasses my world screaming of joy when I accept its world of painful drama. Death loves the hopelessness of my spirit and waits to feed it, eagerly. Together our awareness of one another grows. Death threatens me with the futility of the moment. I stand free in the infinity of my heart. Death reminds me as a dark hood about to cover my head if I am not alert, ready, and willing to risk being separate from its grasp. In my unwillingness to let go, death sings. In my constant rebirth, death is realized for its illusion.

As much as death is my best friend, each day is a beautiful lover. Risking, reaching, allowing my lover, keeps me awakened to my heart, my experience, my initiation into the other. With death as my shadow and the world as my lover, the Shamanic unravels its constant mystery. Death and my lover are always teasing one another for control. My pain grabs me to hold back as love begs me to come to her. Death welcomes my fear as my lover uncovers all of me. Which bed as I going to go towards, the one of pain or joy? Which garden am I going to plant? Each of them exists for my acceptance. But only my lover really exists. Death is the creation of my frightened will doubting my true nature. Love is ready to embrace, hold and caress every part of me, every moment of fear. But I must want her, ask her, and approach her. She is always naked and I must be willing to also be naked. My lover is reaching out her hand and all I have to do is take it. She comes to me in an endless number of ways each day, welcoming me at every turn. But am I willing? Am I willing to simply recognize her? My lover is here and it's only a question of my will. My will? Death or rebirth, death or rebirth, my heart gives bloom to consciousness. Within this secret awaits the Shamanic initiation.

The Heart
of
Trust

One day I was dreaming. I am climbing a mountain approaching a cave. Inside I find a skinny wise yogi sitting in a loin cloth. He is perfectly still, high, full of love. I ask him questions and he answers by just looking at me. I ask him about my lover and he answers by sharing his peace with me. I ask him about my path and he answers by just smiling at me. Every question I think to ask receives a similar response of remembering to trust. He doesn't say anything but in his eyes, I hear him promising everything. Everything awaits in trusting.

A few days later I was at a cabin in the Austrian Alps awakening from a dream. A Unicorn has just flown into my sleep with a big ugly horn menacing my being. I feel off balance and frightened. My friends and I have taken a snow cat ride up to this snowy retreat to run a group for three days. Tall peaks surround us on all four sides. It's morning and I was sitting in bed feeling this heaviness about me which I don't understand.

A few hours later, I had an opportunity to grab a pair of skis, get out and get away from this feeling which persisted A part of me is interrupting my escape reminding me to double check the bindings. But I am not listening, rushing, rushing somewhere. Two quick runs and I am feeling unsure of myself. The snow is hard on top with several inches of soft underneath. Next I'm falling, my leg going over my head, my bindings not releasing, a cracking sound breaks, feeling something in my leg tearing. Everything has stopped. I am just laying in the snow. In the deepest part of myself I know I am asking for help. I am asking that my leg not be broken, that I can return to the lodge. Slowly I stand up refusing to accept being immobolized.

After limping and being carried around that afternoon, I lay in bed, feeling very small, beginning to cry. My eyes seem to let go of the pain as it lets go of tears. Again I am asking for help, trusting for some greater part of me, something beyond me to be with me. I feel myself in a dream, leaving my body, flying back to this cave which is somehow also a cloud and a garden. I hear people in the room about me but I am gone. A little man like my Yogi of a few days before, appears and he gently walks over looking at my knee. Then just as easily, he takes me up inside of my knee showing me how I damaged it. I see a twisted muscle, torn, and something appears chipped underneath. He begins sending intense golden energy into the damage. I see it working. He takes me along a cord of pain into my stomach pointing to the real cause of my accident. I see the unicorn again and my frightened feelings. The little man says, "don't worry about your knee because it will be well when you are well again with your feelings." He leaves and I feel myself returning, opening my eyes only to shut them and fall asleep. There is a beautiful calm.

Again I am dreaming, asking my grandmother, parents, and brothers to pray for me. From a hospital bed I am realizing my separateness from everyone, feeling hopeless. In moments I sense everyone praying for me but I am dieing. I awaken, crying, hysterical, frightened. I do not want to die. I love them all too much. I'm afraid!

A special friend comes over to me and holds me, urging me to go back into the dream. He is telling me that death is not leaving but going to. My whole body is shaking, crying until I am suddenly just aware of his presence, seeing this light blue spirit above me, welcoming me. I'm afraid but gradually go into the blue light. I am not leaving but going into. I am urged to trust my way into the new. A prayer for healing enters and leaves my lips. As long as I am asking and believing in my request, the pain subsides. All night I utter these words. By morning the prayer has changed to the words "faith, faith in healing." These words and the blue light has surrounded me. My knee is much better but stiff.

Inside I find this skinny wise Yogi.
He loves to laugh at me
Reminding me that everything is right
Except when I need to relearn
That everything is perfectly right.

He said: "Don't worry about your knee
Because it will be well
When you are well again
With your feelings."

The more I am hurting
The more he smiles at my questions
The more his eyes promise everything
The more I am when trusting.

Our group work continues. The Alps are an impressive setting for all of us to feel ourselves. Meanwhile everyone is gathering around me. I feel their love. Tears form. The pain in my knee has again started to overwhelm me. I'm crying, letting go, reaching and I am gone again, visiting the little man on the cloud. He just looks at me puzzled, walking around me, thinking, smiling. I am crying for help and by his expression I know he's reminding me of faith. My tears come from a deeper place as I feel my fear. Then the little man comes over, takes me in his arms and holds me. I am completely wrapped in his arms, his love. His body is merging with mine then withdrawing and merging again. The information that I still don't trust enough comes to me as I return to the room realizing I am not ready yet to let go of my injury completely.

Evening, I'm laying in group feeling the love, the intense love in the group. I feel my stomach, my feelings so strong. I'm just surrendering, laughing at the pain. I feel free. Moments later I get up and start walking without crutches. I'm walking around the room with practically no limp and no pain at all. With time my knee finished healing but the pain was gone forever.

A few months later I'm awakened with this feeling of heaviness. Genny and I had been traveling in Italy with our 1963 Mercedes. I knew something was off balance but unsure where to trust. I proceeded through the day ignoring my feeling. Several hours later our Mercedes stopped abruptly on the Italian highway. Immediately my morning feeling is realized and has located itself in my world. The car has suffered some sort of a coronary. I had known something was going to happen all day. Now my feelings make sense and the best choice to make is beginning to trust that the best outcome will come about. Waiting, tow truck, speaking Spanish hoping it is understood as Italian, uncaring mechanics, suitcases in hand, we're finding ourselves having to abandon our car in the Italian countryside. Our way is now on foot and by train. The days grab us with our anxiety and let go with our trust.

A few train rides later we arrive back home in Germany. Doris has come to visit and we are telling her our trials, our dramas of faith. In the midst of discussing language problems and trying to be understood, Doris is asked about her meeting with the Jivaro Indians in South America after the Second World War. She proceeds to tell the story of being warned not to enter the jungles because the Jivaros are cannibals. Many people who strayed into them including a recent group of people from a major oil company, have never returned. But Doris' husband has had a vision of walking on the jungle floors and having their heads as their own. So together they fly, canoe, and finally take a raft deep into Ecuador. As they proceed they feel eyes watching them. Doris and her husband trust their vision and just know from someplace within they are safe. They strip all their clothes, proceeding naked, giving sign that they are leaving all their past, coming without anything but themselves. They smash berries all over their bodies. Offerings and prayers are made to the trees as they eat roots and greens surrounding their campsite. They sleep buried in the sand, still feeling observed.

Upon waking they find trenches dug around their heads. All night they had heard nothing. Inside of the trenches dug six inches down they find berries and herbs. Is all of this a warning of some kind? They decide to eat them taking the food as gifts. Now should they wait or proceed in some direction into the jungle looking for the Indians?

A path is found leading deep into the jungle. They proceed finding every mile or so a dead animal laid on the path in front of them by the Indians. All along they have felt as if they are being watched. Are the animals a warning? Looking closely they see poison darts near each dead animal. Deciding the animals are a guide to pass safely, they bow and continue respectfully with each encounter. Finally they enter a deserted village.

People's eyes are felt observing from the bushes. Doris and her husband sit naked back to back and make low guttural sounds, traditional worship sounds of different tribes she had been a part of in the South Pacific. Animal noises are made and soon the children come out, feeling Doris and her husband as witch doctors. Sitting quietly, Doris erects a tent

The Heart
of
Love

There is a dream that I awaken to where I am surrounded by mountains imposing upon me, demanding me to climb. All the signs about me urge me to stay on the marked paths. People are calling to me to hurry, look here, rest there, pointing out all the turns and places for me to go. Any discouragement I may feel is taken away with great promises of what's to find on the mountain tops. All the slogans say, and most everyone agrees, I will be able to see everything once there. "There" is some vague yet magical spot. I don't quite understand why I should start climbing so I can get to a place to stop again and rest. Nevertheless I feel compelled to climb. No matter how well I stay on the marked paths some part of me feels taken away. Once on top I feel little different than before. But I continue climbing.

Maybe if I get some climbing equipment, go to climbing school, eat climbing food, find the right climbing companion to help me I'll get there. The manuals I see encourage me to do these exercises every morning, think certain thoughts when the going is rough, buy special clothing to lighten my load. Everywhere there seems to be the promise that the going will be easier. There are natural products, books and teachers who will show me some things immediately and greater lessons after years of disciplined devotion to learning how to climb. Hundreds of climbing techniques await me to learn and master. The News tells of climbing success and defeats as I hear of friends discovering wealth and love, poverty and despair. The story sounds for all of them about the same with advice to climb longer, higher, faster, or just better.

In this dream the message is to climb, climb, and climb some more. I am told that as long as I am climbing, trying to get someplace other than I am, everyone around me will be happy. Most everyone seems to be dreaming that if we can be some other place other than where we are—we will be happy.

Relationships provide new paths for climbing. They are the stages for me to act out the surrender and compromises I am experiencing. In this dream growth requires some form of pain, self punishment, as if there are a thousand ways of self surrender and developing one's self which have come to mean the same. Somehow being has come to require a path of looking for more obstacles denying my being.

The dream beckons lovers who enjoy struggle. While climbing, it is difficult to be satisfied with myself no less someone else. Sometimes I am busy turning a friend into a cold and angry parent who I can pin my discomfort to. Other times I am trying to make someone the monster I can attribute all my fears to or the angel that I have been searching for who will save me. While climbing I can't believe I deserve love. My partner must be the monster within my grasp or the angel just out of reach. I cannot imagine my life without struggles, no less begin such a way. I continue the dream, climbing as long as I believe I deserve little more. Sometimes the realization comes that I can feel cared for by another as much as I care for myself. But while climbing, the mountains are full of excuses, indeed the paths teach me ways, not to love myself. I keep going frightened of any change. Whenever I go out looking for another way I simply find myself continuing to climb, trying to get someplace other than I am.

To stop the dream I must decide to begin another. The dream begins by trying not to get anywhere but where I am. One time I literally stopped the action. I was lonely. Instead of climbing, searching for someone who would satisfy my needs I sat under my favorite tree. I was lonely and I told myself it was all right. Just by stopping the search I began to feel better. For the better part of four months I sat under that tree each day feeling it was the best place for me to be. I felt instead of going out into the world trying to make my old girlfriend love me, I was beginning to love myself. I knew she could not give to me any more than what she could give to herself. She knew the most real gift to her was for me to be with me.

The tree and I began to talk to one another, listen and be together. Gradually I began to feel as strong as him as I noticed he did not go out and struggle for air and water. He did not run around looking for the sun. Why should I go looking everywhere? Why not just expect it all, expect love?

By this tree, a beautiful woman began to fill my heart. I felt her growing throughout all of me like branches and leaves reaching out to every limb. I did not know where she came from. But things like where, from and to, questions of how and why seemed part of past dreams of not accepting me right now. All I knew was I was slowly feeling her roots pierce all my being. One day I was sleeping on the grass and she flew into my dream, holding me, expressing her love for me. I awakened and felt totally cared for, by myself and some other. I knew her. She was in my life as any other person had ever been. I knew it would only be time before I would meet her and she would be physically with me. I was trusting my heart to fill up. Asking for her to come into my life, I believe I deserve to feel full.

Soon it was time to leave my tree and the city I was living in. I just knew it. I was in love and knew my old surroundings were not a part of this new affair. I had to let go of the old satisfactions I had in my old ways and trust in the new which was happening. My lover is coming into my life. Dreams told about her. Friends confirmed that they felt her. As much as I trusted my heart to sit and nourish by my tree, I began expecting this spirit that came into my sleep to come into my day. Weeks and months went by as I traveled doing workshops, moving about, always being ready to meet her.

Finally when I had forgotten about meeting her because my heart was bursting, too full to expect more, some extraordinary events began happening.

A week before I was bound for Germany, I walked into a friend's house and met Genny who was exactly like the woman I met months before on the grass in my sleep. We talked for fifteen minutes as my forgotten dream flashed through me. Now however she had to go. Both of us knowing something special had begun we did not quite know the words to accept it. She left and I went on toward Europe crying for joy and for trusting. In hours I would be thousands of miles apart from her but we had already been so together that being apart now somehow could not matter. Everything in me knew she too in some time would be really with me. All I accepted as something to believe had told me the preparation, the process of having this relationship was as important as the relationship itself. My dreams had told me we would meet and travel together long before I knew I would be doing any traveling or had definite knowledge she existed. Here she was and I had to let her go. In Germany I found new spots like my tree before and continued nourishing my awakened heart.

The day she landed to join me everything was new and like memories of long ago. Our fears and doubts quickly passed with the realness of our courses merging. Neither of us had expected yet just the same had expected to find a heart of love. Our dream together quickly went into the midst of angel and magic hunts where the hunting is the most important thing. The beauty of the moments were just unfolding. And ever since almost twenty-four hours every day we have spent together, reminding one another of our dream with trees instead of mountains, learning from one another that the love we realize in the world is the love waiting inside of us to affirm. The hearts of hearts of others are always teaching us to continue.

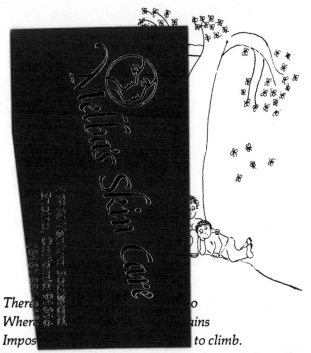

There_____o
Wher_____ains
Impos_____ to climb.
Everyone around me is urging me to be someplace other than I am.

There is this dream that I awaken to
Where I am sitting next to this tree
And know the roots and branches, trunk and leaves
Is me. I am a tree.

There is this dream that I awaken to
Where a beautiful woman begins to fill my heart
I feel her growing throughout all of my
Branches and leaves, reaching out to every limb.

There is this dream that I awaken to
Where I love this dream until I am all of it.
Then together we sit next to our tree and realize
The love we feel in this world.

Is the love waiting inside of us.

The
Garden

What's special about the garden is that it looks exactly how I want it to be. Instead of giving it a design, allowing for its design seems to be the garden's secret. In my heart are my desires, the seeds to my own magic, the miracles to change my life and other's, and the garden to continue growing. Trust unfolds the whole beginning which is always beginning with something new.

Watching my thoughts as they surface, I am watching the limits I attach to my garden. The gate to myself leads to the gate beyond myself. As I become aware of my thoughts I am becoming free of them. Similarly as I become aware of my body I am going beyond my body. The gate is always swinging. It is up to me to slip through and join the Other. The opening to the garden comes between each thought. As my thoughts approach my path the opening grows and grows.

As I understand that my body, all the events and experiences of my life are an extension of my thoughts. My body, my life's events and experiences begin to change as easily as beginning to think about something else.

Instead of the world pushing and pulling me, my will creates my world. Instead of thinking to struggle, my thoughts create and determine my course. Until now all my

107

energy has been invested in believing how powerful the world is and how small my thoughts. As I understand that the world is no bigger than my ability to see it, my life's energy is realized to be nowhere but in myself. The wealth and beauty of the world awaits for me in each tiny thought, like atoms waiting to expand and control. I am constructing my heart.

When I slow my thoughts until one actually stops and I peek around it to see the world, I begin seeing everything as it actually is. The garden bursts forth. Heaven appears on Earth. My Heaven and my Earth appears as I am choosing it to be.

As the reality of my problems merge with the reality of my fantasies, my will merges with the world, Heaven is found on Earth. When I stop looking for my fantasy and my heart, when I stop looking for Heaven always beyond me, I find it waiting just inside. When I am no longer looking for Heaven in the sky, I find Heaven on Earth. Indeed Heaven is waiting on Earth. It always has and always will. As soon as I am ready, I will no longer be apart from myself and Heaven will no longer be apart from Earth.

Meanwhile as I walk in and out of Heaven and Earth, I am learning to recognize the difference. I begin saving little power rocks and fantasies, presents and dreams I find in the garden. Whenever I am lost I have these special objects from the garden as far away as my pocket or my heart to remind me of where I really want to be. In my pocket are the objects from the garden I have picked up and saved. Within my heart are the memories and will, the seeds and the magic waiting for me to be in Heaven on Earth once again.

As painful and overwhelmed I may feel there is the love of all the hugs I have ever received waiting to re-unite with me.

Earth is based upon winning and losing, losses and gains. But as I realize I cannot win and lose my will, I am reminded. The life of struggle is based upon some problems being more difficult than others. But as I realize I am always the same distance from my heart, again I am reminded.

Living on Earth is a process of choosing and holding-

Within the garden there is peace
Because within the garden there are choices
Realizing my choices plants the seeds
For my will to grow and grow into my own. . .

The problem is life's mystery
Being humble enough to ask
Being humble enough to receive.
There seems to be nothing more and so much more.

Instead of loving thy mother and thy father
Instead of loving thy God
Accept thy mother's and thy father's love
Accept God's love

Love is waiting
Always ready
To give me more
If I am willing . . .

onto my most desired fantasies and dreams. Heaven is a process of trusting and letting go for new ones to come. Living in Heaven on Earth I am always holding on and letting go, holding on and letting go, believing I deserve what I want to be happening. Everything is taking place here in the garden. All is waiting along life's path; the garden, the magic, the miracles, all of me in pursuit of my heart. In Heaven On Earth my child never stops growing.

When I stop looking for Heaven
Always beyond me
I find it waiting just
Inside.

When I am no longer looking for Heaven
In the sky
I find Heaven on Earth.
Indeed Heaven is waiting on Earth.

It always has and always will
As soon as I am ready.
I will no longer be apart from myself
And Heaven will no longer be apart from Earth.

Bruce Davis, Ph.D. is also the author of *The Heart Of Healing* and his newest book *My Little Flowers*. Bruce has a unique gift of appreciating and deeply touching the magical child in many people. He offers counseling, healing, and spiritual retreats in many parts of the United States and Europe. In addition, Bruce leads pilgrimages to Assisi, Italy and other sacred places around the world. Besides leading retreats, he enjoys raising his son and supporting friends and many different groups and communities to grow into their unique purpose.

For more information about Bruce's retreats and current activities please write:

Spring Grove
P.O. Box 807
Fairfax, California 94930

"Your happiness is always in relation to how much attention you give to the present moment . . . .Let me take you to my gardens and whisper to your soul. Here my flowers and leaves still can talk to one another without interruption." *My Little Flowers*

Bruce's newest book *My Little Flowers* is a very personal journal which offers us a daily meditation of profound dimensions. Every day love is present asking who is listening, challenging us to receive and enjoy life's little flowers.

"Love has no introduction. Love appears. Love just is. And despite our attempts to manage Her, She wins. If we withdraw, if we surrender, if we call out or if we are silent, She is as we are prepared to know Her. Ordinary or Holy, everywhere we turn love faces us. Again and again, She is here." *My Little Flowers* invites us to our heart of hearts to listen and follow love's direction. Through the simplicity and stillness in each daily meditation, many people are discovering their own deepening spiritual experience.